The Pye Package

The continuing story

Marie Pye

Published 2023
By Mswllbooks Ltd
www.mswallbooks.com
The moral right of Marie Pye to be identified as
the author of this work has been asserted by her
in accordance with the Copyright, Designs and
Patents Act 1988.

All enquiries should be addressed to:
Mswallbooks Ltd
20-22 Wenlock Road, London, N1 7GU

Cover design by M.S. Wall
ISBN: 979-8-859614-72-1
Printed in the UK
V9.00

DEDICATION

A huge thank you to my husband Howard and my daughters Katherine and Alison for all their encouragement in helping me carry on.

Also, thank you to the fellow writers in my creative writing class who listened patiently to my ramblings.

ACKNOWLEDGEMENTS

To Mike Wall, who has helped me believe in myself and my ability to convert my story into a book.

Mike has guided and encouraged me every step of the way, and without his help, this project would never have seen the light of day.

Thank you so much from the bottom of my heart.

CHAPTER 1

Married life begins.

In early 1968, I worked as a secretary at Lynd-Air, based at Tottenham Court Road, London, and was introduced to my future husband by my boss, Harry Walton.

Howard was employed in an advertising agency as an accounts manager. By July 1968, we were married in St. Agnes Catholic church, and after our honeymoon in Pevensey, we returned to London, where my story continues.

We stayed in Howard's bedsitter in Courtfield Garden, Earl's Court.

Courtfield Gardens – Earls Court

The flat consisted of one room with a double bed, a table set by the window, two chairs, a Baby Belling cooker, and a tiny black and white Television. I can't quite remember where we stored our clothes, but they must have been somewhere!

The bathroom doubled as a kitchen. A wooden plank extended across the bath with a washing-up bowl placed on top to act as the sink. There was no drainer to leave clean gear, so washing up was a two-man job. One washed, and the other dried. It was very cosy. I would make dinner every evening, which proved a trifle difficult as I could not cook. However, by the time we married, Howard was twenty-seven and had a fair bit of flat living experience under his belt.

After a few weeks of struggling, I took myself off to Foyles, the famous bookshop on Tottenham Court Road and explained my problem to the assistant. She recommended a book called – All in the Cooking, Part 1.

It was basic and started by telling you to buy the cabbage before cooking it! With my book and Howard's help, I managed pretty well. Back in Dublin, my hometown, we always had dessert or sweets, as we called them. About two months into our marriage, as we chomped our way through the stuffed baked apple with nuts and raisins, Howard looked up at me and said.

"Marie, I don't want to be rude or anything, but I don't really need pudding every evening."

I looked at him in suspended disbelief and yelped for joy. I can remember dancing around the flat with enthusiasm. The prospect of not grappling with a dessert each evening was joyous.

We settled into married life so quickly. Sometimes, we would go out for breakfast on Sunday, reading the papers and repeatedly refilling our coffee cups. 1968 was so decadent. I loved it.

Of course, my pregnancy was the backdrop to all this, and thank God, I had no problems whatsoever. However, it did lead to other chapters in my story.

I worked daily throughout my term, but we still had time to socialise most evenings. Harry Walton, my boss, was a jazz pianist. In his spare time, he played at various venues around London. We often heard him perform and met with others who liked to follow him. It turned out Howard, who sang as a choirboy at the Queen's coronation in 1953, was massively into music, whereas, unfortunately, I was not. Howard was very patient with me as he tried to broaden my knowledge. Early on, he asked.

"Do you like Elgar?"

I genuinely inquired if it was a new brand of cornflakes! I didn't have a clue!

Howard and I also went to the theatre and cinema. It was good fun, and I learned about many new places, people, and bars in London.

Howard's parents, Doreen (Mother) and Bertie (Father), and his two brothers, Nigel and Rupert, lived in Chipstead, Surrey. The house was called West Winds and stood on over an acre. Father kept the garden like Kew. I swear each blade of grass was the same length. It was beautiful to look at but endless work. We were often invited to Sunday lunch, a grand affair with the best Silver on show. Mother was very good to us, and Rupert drove us home to Earls Court at the end of the evening. It was a way Mother kept an eye on us without us even noticing!

When I finished work in early February 1969, I was the size of a house. In those days, there were no rules about eating, drinking, and smoking during pregnancy and no such thing as maternity leave. The baby was due at the end of the month, and married women were expected to stay home to look after their child. At first, I accepted the situation as it was the norm, but as you will read later, things changed.

Our bed-sit was unsuitable for the baby, and I doubt the landlord would have even entertained the idea. I do not remember being stressed by the situation and just going with the flow. Howard's mother saw some new two-bedroom flats being built in Whyteleafe. They were set in a leafy area with easy access to Whyteleafe and Upper Warlingham stations. We went for it. Both Dads gave us £250 each for the deposit. Howard's mother was very astute and insisted we also buy the garage. It was such a good move.

We were successful, and over the last couple of months of my pregnancy, we tried to get it ready for the baby. We were given a cot, a Pye family heirloom, and painted it yellow, as we did not know if we were having a boy or a girl. However, we did buy a new mattress.

In those days, the government gave us a universal grant of £25. Everyone got it, and we used it to buy a Silver Cross pram, which was the order of the day.

33 Hillside Road Whyteleafe

When I entered the doors of St. Mary Abbot's Hospital on 25th February 1969, I was like a waddling duck. I waited and waited and waited. On the morning of 26th February, my waters broke. Naively, I thought that was it. The baby would pop out any minute.

You guessed. Not a bit of it! There was no question of anybody being with you and no such thing as a birthing partner. Howard was at work and could only see me during official visiting hours. I was on my own the whole day, in dreadful pain, having contractions, screaming, bawling, and shouting. It was not a pretty sight. When visiting hours finished, Howard had to leave, and I was placed in a room with Matron at one end and me at the other. As Howard went out of the door, Matron said.

"Don't bother ringing up until the morning, Mr. Pye, as nothing will happen this evening."

I always had a dramatic streak in me and shouted.

"If I am still here in this state in the morning, I will die."

Howard duly left, and my darling Katherine was born at 9.10 p.m. I somehow knew I could not go through the night. It was the most wonderful feeling in the whole world when she was placed in my arms. Incredibly, all the pain was forgotten. A wonderful nurse said she would phone Howard on her way home. What an angel. However, he was still not allowed to visit until morning.

He arrived as early as possible and was ecstatic to see our baby. Even though we did not know if we were having a boy or a girl, we already had a name for her: Katherine Mary. My grandmother was called Catherine, and Howard's mother said she did not care what we called her, so all sides were suited.

Later in the day, Howard went off to announce Katherine's birth in the Telegraph newspaper.

I was in the hospital for ten days. Breastfeeding did not come easy, or should I say, it did not come at all. The nurses kept saying it was because I had the wrong nursing bra. Really! Howard was duly dispatched to Bourne and Hollingsworth department store in Oxford Street to make a purchase. I do not remember the exact price, but they were each an arm and a leg. However, I drew the line when the nurse tried to give Howard size instructions to buy a third one. We could not take the others back as they were soaked in milk after even one unsuccessful attempt. Nursing bras are hilarious as well as challenging to manage. In the end, I switched to a bottle. Phew, what a relief.

Looking back, Howard's mother was extremely helpful and nurtured us during the pregnancy. However, very early on, she said.

"Do not buy anything for the baby."

Which meant, of course, I didn't.

When she collected us from the hospital and took us back to Whyteleafe, which was quite a journey, she asked if I had any bottles to feed Katherine.,

"No," I replied, "you said not to buy anything!"

How naïve I was. Given that start, it's incredible how well Katherine has done. We stopped at a chemist and got sorted.

Mother was very helpful and steered us through Katherine's first few months. I was consumed with unconditional love and a sense of responsibility for the little person relying on me. Katherine and Howard were my family.

We were the first people in the Whyteleafe flats to have a baby! Which meant there was nobody to compare notes with.

CHAPTER 2

Settling into a routine with Katherine

Initially, I wondered if I was approaching motherhood correctly. I got through each day but questioned everything. The constant process of feeding, changing, and washing was exhausting. Katherine was a poor sleeper, which did not help my general equilibrium. I now know I had mild post-natal depression, which was not a recognised medical condition in those days. It was just called the baby blues and almost entirely dismissed. I didn't really question it. I thought it was all part of having a baby. Not knowing anybody in the area did not help. I couldn't ring my Mam and worry her. I remember going to Whyteleafe Park, sitting on a bench, and feeling utterly isolated and exhausted! Occasionally, I would chat to another Mum and regale how I had been pacing the floor in our lounge all night. I told them we would soon have wheel marks up the middle of the carpet we bought on the never-never.

Although Howard's mother watched over me, I leaned heavily on Howard during this period. It never even vaguely occurred to me to go to the doctor. How times change.

Howard had to go to work, and I was left to get on with it. The days were long, I did not know anyone, and I felt down in the mouth. Howard and I were chatting one evening, and he suggested I find a library. I felt there was little chance of one being in Whyteleafe, but I gave it some thought over the next few days. Determined to do something more positive, I popped Katherine into the pram and physically searched. To my surprise and delight, I found a library just past the railway station. It was small but cosy.

As I opened the door, Hannah, the librarian, met me. She was very welcoming and extremely helpful. I remember spending ages there, and just as I was about to leave, I asked her about a book for my husband.

"What kind of books does he like?" She asked.

"Blood, sex and violence, preferably with a swastika on the front," I replied.

At this time, I had no idea Hannah was Jewish. As it transpired, it did not matter. She made me a cup of tea the following week, and our slow-burning friendship started. It lasted for over forty years, during which time I relied heavily on her guidance and influence. Hannah died at Ninety-three, and we were friends until the end.

Homemade Hannah at Home 1984

Finding Hannah was life-changing. I had always been an avid reader. Visiting the library and joining 'story time' on Friday afternoon became a social event. At the same time, learning that other mums had similar experiences with young children was very cathartic. At last, I knew I was not alone.

It was probably the launching pad which enabled me to move forward. To look outwards and not feel sorry for myself. There was life out there!

We had a thing called a swap shop in the village. One Saturday morning, Howard took his camera down to swap it.

Let me fill you in: this was a fancy camera in a leather case, with wonderful lenses and all the bells and whistles. The only thing it did not seem to do was take photos. It had eaten our honeymoon snaps and every photo from Katherine's birth. I suggested to Howard it was useless, and he agreed. He exchanged it for an LP of The Enigma Variations by Elgar. With this, my dip into the wide musical world began.

Children do not come with a manual! The early months were difficult, and I was learning on the job, getting on the best I could. Everything was so new. As Katherine grew bigger, I slipped further into motherhood. I enjoyed going to the park and the library but did not know anybody else with children. The days were long until Howard returned from work. The washing was particularly difficult. It all had to be done by hand in the bath or sink, although I did have a washboard, which made things a little easier. Of course, there were no such things as disposable nappies, which meant you always had to have a constant supply of laundered ones ready. The flat had no drying facilities, so wet clothes were draped everywhere. They were only hand-wrung and took ages to dry. When we could afford it, we graduated to a clothes horse, and as we were on the ground floor, I could put it outside.

When Katherine was about four months old, Howard announced he used to play cricket for a club in Caterham. It was news to me. I knew absolutely nothing about the game and was both excited and intrigued. The following Saturday, we headed up to the Club. It was quite a hike, pushing the pram up Burntwood Lane. Howard was greeted like a long-lost brother, even though he had not played for some time. It turned out he was both a wicketkeeper and an opening batsman. We stayed all afternoon and had a great time. When we were about to leave, I nearly tripped over this thing lying in the grass.

"What's this?" I asked.

"It's a box," he replied.

"Don't be ridiculous. It has not got a lid," was my response.

Everyone howled with laughter and had to explain its function in detail. I was not amused and felt like a right fool.

Throughout the summer, Howard played the odd game, and I would come up to watch some of it. A match would last a long time, and it was difficult with Katherine being so young. There were no other children, and it was all a bit blokey, so I was never very encouraging. Really, I preferred it when he did not play.

During this time, my brother Colman lived in London, where he met and married a lovely French girl called Christiane. Her parents lived in the South of France, but they came to London for their wedding. I invited them to Whyteleafe for dinner and was able to practice my French.

Coleman and his new wife regularly joined us for Sunday lunch. I loved entertaining, and it improved my cooking. Colman often helped as he was a bit of a dab hand in the kitchen. Christiane adored children and would play with Katherine for ages. When she took her for a bath, Katherine emerged looking like an advertisement for Pears Soap. Unfortunately, they moved to Dublin before Alison was born.

Harry Walton, our best man, was also a regular visitor for Sunday lunch. By then, he had split up from his wife and played the field. It meant we were subjected to each of his new girlfriends for approval. It was hilarious, and I loved it. It brought a whole new dimension to my life.

Harry was well into his fifties and a larger-than-life character. He eventually married a girl many years younger than himself. They had two children and settled down in a place called Battle. We remained friendly with his new family and would visit Sussex to see them. My geographical knowledge of Britain was limited, so visiting new places was great.

Unfortunately, when Harry's children were about three and one, he had a tragic accident mowing the grass and electrocuted himself.

As Harry was a jazz pianist, about seventy musicians attended his funeral and started a jamming session. I had never seen anything quite so spontaneous in my whole life. It was glorious and the send-off he so deserved. Howard was working abroad at the time, so he could not attend. Alison came with me. She was seven or eight by then, and it was her first funeral.

In Katherine's first year, we took her to Ireland to show her off!! My Mam, Aileen, and Nellie, our family housekeeper, looked after her for a few days while Howard and I took off to Kerry on a camping holiday. It was all borrowed equipment, and Mam lent us her car. We camped on the beach and in farmer's fields; lo and behold, we had no rain on this trip. It was a pure miracle. We adored Katherine, but having a break was joyous.

Every mother I know who is semi-normal seems to feel the same. Howard and I had a riotous time, and the freedom was awesome. We went to places I had never been to in Kerry and realised what a beautiful country Ireland was. Breath-taking skies and roaring oceans.

To this day, I adore the sound of the sea and the foamy white horses riding on top of the waves.

128 Phibsborough Road

After five days, we were refreshed and ready to return to 128 Phibsborough Road. Katherine was sitting in the front garden in her borrowed pram, hair combed in a bit of a quiff and beaming from ear to ear, just watching the traffic and passers-by. Very memorable.

In contrast to Ireland, when Katherine was a toddler, Howard's parents took us on holiday to Swanage in Dorset. I had never been caravanning before, and quite frankly, I hated it. Maybe it was because we were all squashed in together, even though the caravan was spacious, as caravans go. My main recollection of the intimate living experience was the washing-up facilities. They were the size of a washing-up basin in a doll' house. Just another thing to contend with! Despite this, Howard's parents were very generous to take us and cough up the rental. So, thank you for that and for introducing us to the beauty of Dorset.

Although I did not enjoy my first caravan experience, Harold and I now love them and are pleased to confirm we are the proud owners of our second caravan on our third site in Rose Green, East Sussex.

My life, however, changed dramatically when I discovered my neighbour, Maureen Rumbold, was pregnant. I kept looking at her, thinking – is she? or isn't she? Everyone in those days who was pregnant received milk tokens. I sneaked over on Saturday morning to check her milk bottles. Eureka, she was. I was over the moon. I approached her that weekend, and our friendship began. We had coffee mornings, chats, and visits to the park. Her baby, Paul, arrived six months later. Over the coming months, more children were born in the Whiteleafe Hillside Road community, and I settled further into the family routine. At the time, I didn't realise relocating to England, getting married, and having a child was such a huge life-changing event. But, all things considered, I do not think I did too badly.

My friendship with Maureen was another slow burner, but it improved my life immensely. When Katherine was about one year old, Maureen and I were chatting and decided our lives would be further enhanced if we could find part-time work. Her husband, Ron, worked at the Post Office and came home at the same time every evening. It enabled them to have a fixed routine, which was everything to them. On the other hand, Howard came home at different times, which meant our family life was comparatively disorganised. In hindsight, I suspect this was also the period Howard started drinking, but I made no connection at the time. I longed for some of Maureen's family stability and realised somehow, I would have to start earning. It took a while, but eventually, I set up an Avon round.

Becoming an Avon representative

It took a long time to establish and a lot of hard work, involving a considerable amount of cold calling. One of my best customers, Liz Ball, who wore piles of makeup, started to take my catalogue to work, which gave me many more orders. It also gave me the idea to leave a catalogue with each of my customers and then return to collect it a few days later. This increased my customer base nicely and enabled me to build a very respectable business. I found it a lot of fun and enjoyed the social interaction with my clients. I started to save for a car and put every penny into our bank account, which grew slowly but steadily.

The Avon round was how I also met Margret Mace. Like me, she was from Dublin and came from a grocery background. We had a lot in common, and she became a good customer. Her daughter, Helen, was a little younger than Katherine, and it was not long before we were on a cup of tea footing. She did not live in the flats. Having a pal further afield seemed adventurous, broadening my network. It was exciting. Margaret was a stay-at-home mum, so it meant we could meet during the day and bounce ideas off each other. We both smoked like troopers, always finding enough money for ten fags. We sat in her kitchen, putting the world right while Katherine and Helen played in the garden. Chatting with my friends was my lifeline.

During one chat session with Maureen Rumbol, the subject of getting paid employment came up again. We got carried away and decided we could job-share, a relatively new concept in those days. We both had office experience and could do most things, from making tea to shorthand, typing, and everything in between. We even agreed she preferred the morning while I liked afternoons. The seed was sown.

Over the weekend, the Rumbolds took off for a short break. Determined to follow through, I took the opportunity, popped Katherine into the pushchair and set off on a mission up Brighton Road, where several factories existed. I went into the first one and asked reception if they had any vacancies. No luck.

Smedley's, which canned fruit and vegetables, was my second try. The girl in reception looked after Katherine while I went upstairs for an interview with a bloke called Andy. I waxed lyrical about my skills, and he said:

"Right, you can have the job of general dog's body at £20.00 a week." Yes, it was the job description he used.

It was good money at the time. I don't remember feeling nervous. Just determined to secure more money somehow. Of course, I was thrilled to be offered the job, but I had not yet mentioned to him the brave Maureen.

"Fantastic," I said, "but there is one little problem. I have a child and can only do half days."

Before he could speak, I jumped in with, "However, I have a mate who could do the other half."

I pumped Maureen's qualities beyond measure and said things like if one of us is sick, the other can cover, and Maureen loved early mornings. The clincher was when I said we could do it for £18 instead of £20. The deal was done.

I hopped out of the factory like a bunny on speed and could not wait to tell Howard and then Maureen on her return from holiday. I was euphoric over the whole weekend.

Disaster. Maureen announced she was not serious and wasn't sure whether Ron would agree. I was devastated. We only had a couple of days before we were due to start at the factory. I begged her to give it a go. We were scheduled to begin a week's trial on the coming Thursday!

It was a huge success and worked a treat. Our only problem was while we were childminding, we had no means of taking the two children out together, which was a bit of a problem. I was aware of a clapped-out double pushchair in the front garden of one of my Avon customers. It had no hood, and one wheel was missing. I knocked on the door and asked Sonia Lewis if we could have it.

"Certainly," she said. Chuffed to be rid of it.

Ron was very practical. He acquired a wheel and painted the pushchair a blue-grey colour. Within a week, Katherine and Paul were being transported around like royalty. Mind you, it still did not have a hood, so we only went out in good weather. The work arrangement suited us both admirably, and we quickly dovetailed into our new job. I never remember any fracas.

Smedley had five factories, and dealing with them made me interested in the geography of Britain. Howard was very knowledgeable about such things, and I hankered to visit different places. I purchased an atlas, and my car project suddenly became more important. I just knew it would enhance our family life.

The double pushchair went everywhere—Croydon on the train, the park in Whyteleafe, the Avon round and the coffee mornings. Katherine and Paul played happily together and got on like a house on fire. Maureen taught Katherine to read, but Paul struggled. It took him until he was ten, plus a good dose of Fungus the Bogey by Raymond Briggs before it clicked. Then he was away.

Howard was a good dad and helped to look after Katherine. Mind you, I never remember him changing her nappy. Apart from not sleeping well, Katherine was an easy kid. She ate and played, and life was uncomplicated. The lack of money, however, was still an issue. I wouldn't say we were extravagant in any shape or form, but we did not have enough to make ends meet. Even with Smedley's money, we never had much left over.

Howard and I talked constantly, and I felt we were open and honest. Katherine was coming up to her second birthday, and we decided to try for another baby on the basis we would somehow manage. Within weeks, I was pregnant. My second pregnancy was very straightforward. By this time, smoking was frowned upon, and I gave it up just like that. I do not remember it being a trial, but I always knew I would return to the habit once the baby was born. I continued job sharing with Maureen at Smedley's and worked up to three weeks before Alison was born in October 1971.

Howard lost his job in the preceding June. This was at least the third time since we were married, but he usually managed to get another quickly. Not this time. We had booked a holiday in Ireland for July and decided if he had not got another job by then, we would move to Ireland permanently, and he would find work there. What a decision, but I was more than happy with it. I did not do too much forward planning in those days. Life was very much on a wing and a prayer.

The day dawned, and there was still no job. We set off to Ireland with blind determination, taking the train from Euston to Holyhead and then the boat to Dublin.

It was an adventure for the three of us—Howard, Katherine, and me, six months pregnant. I had told my parents Howard was searching for a job. Mam was delighted we were coming over and didn't think Howard would have difficulty getting work.

My family in Ireland was always busy as my Da, Michael, owned a shop at the other end of Phisborough Road, and my sister Therese lived up the road in Glasnevin with her husband, Vincent Flynn. Everyone was constantly up and down to the store while Nellie was in the house with permanent cups of tea.

As July merged into August, Therese and I decided to take a holiday house in Skerries for the month. It is only eighteen miles from Dublin, so again lots of toing and froing.

It was easy for Howard to nip up and down for networking and job hunting. The year before I moved to England, I worked in the Irish advertising industry, so I put out feelers again to see if anything was happening.

In the meantime, we continued holidaying, but the weather was awful. It rained every day. However, we still had lots of fun with board games, walks with raincoats and cooking. Of course, everybody frequently came to visit, so cooking became a theme.

Katherine and Cousin Paul (Therese's boy) at Skerrie 1971

Howard could make a mean macaroni cheese, which we all loved and still do. During one of these rainy days, he decided to make one of his specials. People were constantly dropping in and out of the holiday house, so he had to keep adding to his pot. We ended up with ten of us, and huge portions were needed! However, in shock and horror, everyone, bar us, hated it. It seems they thought we were having sweet macaroni pudding. Savoury Mac and Cheese had not reached Irish menus in 1971.

Meanwhile, the rain continued every single day. On the 30th of August, before going to bed, I said to Therese,

"I don't care what the weather brings tomorrow; it's our last day, and we are going to the beach."

The day dawned, and yes, you guessed, it was raining. It had been 30 days on the trot! Undaunted, we wrapped ourselves up to the gills and went to the seaside. With Granny Pye's coat around my bump, sitting on the stones, I tried to stay positive, but the elements defeated us. We returned to the house within thirty minutes to pack up and say goodbye to Skerries and our extremely soggy holiday.

Howard continued to look for work. He explored every possible avenue to no avail. He even ended up doing my father's milk round. One week went into another, and I was getting nearer and nearer to the birth of our second baby. Fortunately, my pregnancy was going well with no problems. Thank God.

It was only four weeks before my due date, and money was still scarce. We decided Howard would continue his quest for employment in the Emerald Isle while Katherine and I returned to our flat in London.

My Mam was worried about how I would fare going back alone. She asked Nellie, our trusted housekeeper, if she would accompany us. Of course, Nellie agreed—such a generous gesture on everyone's part.

Nellie looked after us as we settled back at Hillside Road, and I set about trying to get some money from the social security people. Endless forms and a couple of visits to the council offices in Caterham produced nothing. I kept trying, and eventually, the council arranged to visit us to check on our home circumstances. No specific time was given, so we were on tenterhooks waiting for the knock on the door. Of course, we did not want them to meet Nellie. Having a housekeeper with me would hardly have qualified me for any handouts. Putting our heads together, we hatched a plan. When they arrived, I would answer the door slowly, giving Nellie time to hide under the bed. Nellie was a very short lady, so she was a good fit. We told Katherine not to say a word (a tall ask for a two-year-old!) Two ladies arrived and went over the place with a fine toothcomb. My heart was pounding for fear of Nellie's discovery. Thank God all passed off smoothly, and we ended up with enough money to get by.

After two weeks, Nellie returned home. Still not a flicker of a job for Howard, and he remained in Dublin. Throughout this period, Howard's mother was very supportive. After much discussion, I agreed to move into West Winds. Just for a couple of days before I went to the hospital so she could look after Katherine.

On the 15th of October 1971, I went to Redhill Hospital in Surrey to have Alison. I was desperately missing Howard by this stage and really wanted him to be with me. I was a huge 13st 7lbs. My hands were swollen, and I had to remove my wedding ring. Howard's mother was terrified people would think I was an unmarried mother and insisted I wear hers, which was larger. At the time, I was non-plussed, but thinking about it now, it was so sweet.

I was admitted around 11:00 a.m., and contractions started at 1:00 p.m. It was nothing as difficult as Katherine's birth. They often say the second baby is easier! I remember listening to Woman's Hour to an item on Dame Flora Robson, and out she popped at 2.50 p.m. She was born with the cord around her neck, but this was sorted out quite quickly. However, it left her a bit blue in the face. We had chosen the name Rosalind, but somehow it didn't suit her.

There I was with my beautiful baby girl, no name or husband, wondering what would happen. However, I had the same glorious euphoric feeling as at Katherine's birth. Unconditional love is so amazing! I asked the nurse for the pay phone, and I rang Ireland and spoke to Howard, telling him our fantastic news. I was on a high and desperately wanted him to return to our little family. I asked him to catch the boat in the evening, which he did; as it turned out, it was one of life's better decisions.

CHAPTER 3

Life with Alison and Katherine

Alison and I were only in the hospital for two days instead of the ten days with Katherine. Upon leaving, I joined Howard and Katherine with his parents in West Winds. It was decided we would all remain there for a couple of weeks to give us time to get used to the new baby. In the '70s, new mothers were treated with kid gloves.

I was confined to bed and told not to go down the stairs. Consequently, I was waited on hand and foot for the first two days. Howard went to London on the third day, networking to get a job. He came home quite squiffy in the evening and had a run-in with his parents. It was all kicking off downstairs whilst I was stuck upstairs! All very unpleasant and awkward, to say the least! When I woke up the following morning, I decided we would return to Whyteleafe to be together as our family.

We told Howard's mother and asked her if she would give us a lift home. She refused. We were totally shocked. I told Howard we would get a cab, which was unheard of then. Howard's mother said we couldn't leave as I could not go down the stairs. Women were not supposed to do stairs after childbirth! It's an absolute myth, as we now know, but everyone bought into it in 1971.

Determined to go, I got Howard to phone Dr Davies, our family doctor in Whyteleafe, for his opinion. He gave his permission. I was instructed to go gently and take it easy. Mercifully, our flat was on the ground floor. We had to call a cab in Whyeleafe, as Howard's mother would not let us use the local taxi firm in case any of the neighbours got a whiff of what was happening, which was ridiculous. Not daunted, we managed to get a taxi and made it home. I was as happy as a pig in muck.

There was no sound from Chipstead, but I didn't care. I had my bloke and my two girls. After a few days, we decided to paint the halls in the flat and smarten things up. So much for taking it easy!

One evening, while this was happening, we heard a noise at the door but no doorbell. Cautiously investigating it, we opened the hall door and discovered all the baby gear we had left at West

Winds. It was all beautifully washed and ironed. Mountains of it, including loads of terry towelling. There were no such things as disposable nappies in those days. Howard's parents had not bothered to knock, and I could not believe how petty they were.

The family settled into a nice little routine, painting and decorating while getting used to two kids instead of one. We were very happy. Howard did an excellent job with the decorating while going up and down to London in search of work. Within a month, he succeeded, which was brilliant.

Alison was a very contented baby and slept so well that I would creep into the bedroom and peep into the carrycot to ensure she was still alive. With Katherine, I was very much feeling my way. However, with Alison, I thought I had a better idea of what I was supposed to do. I was much more relaxed. Katherine loved her and wanted her to sit up as soon as possible so she could play with her.

Margaret Mace had her second child, Richard, in July. We became even closer. Howard settled into the new job, and I got on with my life. Through my Avon round, which I continued doing, I got to know many new people. More babies were born on Hillside Road, so there were more stay-at-home mums, which was brilliant for Maureen and me. Weeks flew by, and we were all getting used to our new families. Howard was back at work, going to London every day. The kids were great, so I took the bull by the horns and called Howard's mother to invite her over. She banged the phone down on me. Wow, how dreadful.

My own mother, Aileen, used to tell us as kids.

"Never come down to the level of the other person."

"Thank you, Mam", I said to myself as I kicked the thought into touch. Doreen was grossly unfair. Fortunately, she rang back in about 20 minutes and, very frostily, said she had decided to pay us a visit. Even then, I felt well towards her. I treated her normally when she arrived and even thanked her for the washing.

Doreen already adored Katherine, but when Alison was in her arms, she melted, and I realised she would miss out on so much if she didn't visit. After this, she dropped by regularly. She would take us all to Sainsbury's in Purley, which was a big smoke. Sainsbury's seemed so sophisticated and huge to me in those days.

Occasionally, we would go further afield to Croydon and places like Kennards and Allders, which were massive department stores. It was slightly more complicated with two children, but we managed fine between the pair of us. Doreen would return to No 33 for a cup of tea and biscuit and help the kids. We gradually settled back into some sort of relationship. We accepted each other for what the situation was. She was Howard's mother, and I loved Howard. Toleration was the order of the day.

Doreen was so different from my own Mam, thank God. I think I put many problems down to Doreen being part of the English stiff-upper-lip brigade. However, she did many good things for us and, in her own way, helped my education in the world's ways. She was a highly intelligent woman, perhaps ahead of her time.

During one of Doreen's visits, she announced she would buy us a washing machine. I cannot say how much it meant to me. Until then, every single stitch of clothes was hand-washed in the bath. How did I wring the water out of them? God only knows. It is utterly amazing what you can do when you must. Off we went to Streatham to a second-hand shop. Somehow, she had sourced a twin tub.

I felt I had hit the big time. It was incredibly generous of Doreen, and I can only say it changed my life beyond measure.

Alison with Granny Pye 1973

Grandpa Pye with Alison and Katherine, 1973

CHAPTER 4

Engagement

When I met Howard, he was already engaged. During our courtship, I learned this was his third time. How did I feel about this? Honestly, it didn't touch me, as I never wanted to get engaged.

Before I left Ireland, the norm was for girls over eighteen (or younger) to look for a bloke with marriage in mind. It sounds ridiculous now, but you were classified 'left on the shelf' by twenty. I didn't hold with this ever since I went to the wedding of one of my cousins who was married just before her nineteenth birthday. I remember waving her off on her honeymoon, thinking there must be more to life than becoming a housewife before you are twenty. I wanted more and to experience life.

I worked in three different types of offices before coming to England. However, my experiences with the girls I worked with were identical. On Monday morning, a girl would come to work flashing a ring. Then came months and months of dresses, flowers, venues, best man, etc. What got me in these scenarios was money was never discussed. It seemed lavish weddings were the order of the day, regardless of the debt incurred. I'm not saying everyone went into debt, but a lot did. Sometimes, it forced them to return to living with one set of parents. This, to me, was one of the worst things in the world. I had a simple wedding and got married in green. I rest my case. Howard's mother, so conventional, was always remarking we never got engaged. Every time she said this, I shrugged my shoulders and moved on. One day, she produced this cute dress ring with a green stone, which she said was an emerald. It had belonged to Howard's grandmother, which made it special. She was long since dead by this time. Funnily enough, I have always liked rings and took to this one immediately. The only problem was the setting was vertical instead of horizontal and wouldn't fit beside my wedding ring.

"You can get it turned around," said the brave Doreen.

I duly took the ring to five different jewellers to get the job done, and they all said more or less same. It was a Victorian ring, and it was too difficult to change the setting. In several cases, they said the stone was glass, and they had put a piece of silver paper behind it to make it shine. Some said the stone was paste and warned it would likely break up if touched. I was disappointed each time I got the news. I told them I didn't care, but nobody wanted to take the risk. Eventually, I gave up on the idea, and it lay in a drawer for ages. I forgot about it until one day, I was getting a watch battery from a funny little jeweller in a garage. He was an old-fashioned bloke, and as he was installing the battery, I thought this geezer might do the ring. I explained the ring's problems, and he said he would look at it. He did a fabulous job, and I was delighted with it. I just stuck it on my ring finger, no ceremony or anything. I wear it every day, and I love it.

CHAPTER 5

College life

I was around Margaret Mace's house one Sunday evening with the kids. Howard was off playing golf. A friend of theirs was visiting, a bloke with four children. After the preliminary introductions, I asked him where his wife was. He explained she was studying for her finals at Maria Grey Teacher Training College in Twickenham. It was a lightbulb moment.

I was so excited to hear all about it, and I asked if I could ring his wife, which I did the next day. She was none too friendly, but she gave me the details. I went through the application process and was successful. It was a part-time course spread over four years, and I was thrilled to bits.

I started in September 1973, just as Katherine joined St Francis Primary School in Caterham. I only had to attend on Tuesday and Thursday evenings for the first year. This suited me admirably as I was around during the day for the kids. Katherine settled into primary school well, and I could spend quality time with Alison alone during the day. We knew more people with children, and meeting up made motherhood enjoyable. Learning from each other's experiences was invaluable.

By this time, I had managed to buy a small second-hand car, a red Ford Estate. During college, I met several new friends, including Janet and Wendy, whom I am still friendly with forty-five years later.

There was also Veronica Hyrciuk, who lived on my road and turned up on my course. We had discussed her doing teacher training at a coffee morning, and she decided to give it a go. In my second year, I met Robyn Gordon, an Australian. She had a kid the same age as Alison and lived, would you believe it, on Gordon Avenue, near the college. She also had a great accent, and I remember her well.

Towards the backend of the 2nd year, Veronica, Robyn, and I decided to get an Au Pair to look after the kids at Robyn's house while we were in lectures. This worked brilliantly. The girl was an Australian whom Robyn already knew. She absolutely loved Alison, Dominic, Alexander, and Karen. They got to do all kinds of creative experiences, giving us the freedom to do our college commitments without time restrictions.

College was a fantastic experience, and being in my thirties, I feel I appreciated it more than if I had gone earlier. I grew in confidence and was subjected to new things all the time. Veronica and I travelled together, which meant we had each other for support and companionship. One night, on our way home, we both felt very peckish. Takeaway food was coming on stream and was very much a treat. We gathered our coins and got a K.F.C.; we barely had enough money! It is the only time I've had it, and I can still taste its deliciousness. Mind you, I have had many other brands of junk food since, but in those days, it was one of life's luxuries.

London is one of the most vibrant cities in the world. Veronica's husband was the art buyer for Harrods, which, of course, I thought was very exotic. One afternoon, she put a note in my letterbox saying she had two free tickets for the Royal Opera House that evening. It was to see King Priam by Michael Tippett. I didn't get to London very often, but it was always so exciting when I did. Funnily enough, I still feel the same way now.

As my parents were such theatregoers, I felt they would be disappointed in me if I didn't visit the London Royal Opera House. So off I went to Covent

Garden. I was in awe and wonderment at the sumptuous, opulent, and luxurious interior of the Opera House. The opera started, and it was in English. I was flabbergasted as I naïvely thought all operas were in Italian.

The only other opera I had ever seen was when I lived in Paris and saw Tosca. Although I did not know the story, I bought a cheap seat in a box in the Gods. It was full of American students who told dirty jokes the whole evening. I left the opera house none the wiser about the story of Tosca. However, I did love the costumes and singing.

Unlike me, Howard is very musical and listens to a wide variety of music but never opera. The evening at the ROH was such an eye-opener, and I began to pay opera singing a lot more respect. When something came on the radio opera-wise, I was somehow moved.

Howard's musical sessions were always mixed in with copious amounts of alcohol, so I tended not to get involved if I could manage it. I would switch off and never really listen. Fortunately, this was not the same for Katherine and Alison; they are both heavily into all genres of music to this day.

Meanwhile, back to college life. Two field trips, one to Paris and one to Wales. These aimed to broaden my experiences and enhance the curriculum I could bring to the classroom.

Paris: - I was so excited to return after sixteen years, having lived there from 1963 to 1965. There was absolutely no structure whatsoever to the course. I was shocked by this but soon devised a plan. However, don't get me wrong, I was pleased to return and revisit all my old haunts.

The tutor took us to our hotel and said, "See you all in three days". It meant we had time to do exactly what we wanted. It took me a while to realise there was no work to be done. A complete skive, all paid for by the college. It was a terrible waste of resources, in my opinion. I was in a gang of three who had never been to Paris. So, we set about exploring literally everywhere. We bought a carnet of tickets for the metro, and I showed them how it all worked. We set about visiting the sights. I feel the best way to get the measure of a place is to walk it if possible. We had a little wander down to 53, Rue de Lisbonne, where I once lived as an au pair. It was just down from the Arc de Triomphe. I had a ball, but I remember one of the girls, was quite a moaner and certainly not a walker. Very frequently, she would get an attack of the vapers and have to go back to the hotel and have a bath. I thought this was outrageous in the middle of the day, no less! The second time this happened, we let her return alone. I probably learnt a good life lesson: not to be a wimp and try to embrace every new experience with gusto.

We went to a few folk clubs, which made me feel like I was back to being a teenager again. It was a great trip and did me a lot of good. Here I was, the kids and husband free for the first time in ages. I grew confident and enjoyed making decisions when I didn't have to consider the family's position or ideas.

The trip was terrific. However, I remember on the way home having trouble with my Irish passport and being held up at the airport, to the annoyance of the rest of the students. It was also in the middle of the I.R.A. Troubles.

Wales: - In my 3rd year, I chose to go on an environmental field studies trip to Wales. I knew little about nature and thought it would be good for me! Once again, I was thrown into the deep end with very little training.

On the first morning, I was sent out and given a stretch of hedge to analyse. However, I did not know the difference between hawthorn and clover!! I spied a telephone box at the crossroads and phoned Howard. He tried to talk me rationally through the situation. After the call finished, I stepped back and reviewed my predicament. There was another girl about half a mile up the road doing her study. After thirty minutes of staring at my new wellies (specially bought for the trip), I gathered courage and joined her. She had done a cross-section drawing with coloured labels. Very elaborate, as I recall, whilst my notebook remained blank.

She showed me how to look at leaf structure, colour and size. It was a whole new world for me, but she was kind and seeing how useless I was, she took pity on me. She got me doing some writing in my notebook, but not so many drawings. I have always been bad at art. There's not an ounce of talent in my bones. When I taught in the reception class in Margaret Roper, I would attempt to draw a house or a little stickman on the blackboard. After letting the kids look at my feeble sketches, I quickly rubbed them out and told them they were much better at drawing than me, which was entirely accurate. I obliterated my efforts because I didn't want any adult who visited the classroom to think I had let the kids draw on the blackboard, which, of course, would not have been politically correct.

Returning to the Ecology Centre, the tutor, who was a no-nonsense guy, gave us each a small cage after supper. The idea was, at dusk, you went out in the woods and set your trap to catch a mammal like a vole, rat, shrew etc. In the morning, you went out to see what had been captured and put nail varnish on the tail to check if they had been caught more than once. I freaked out in my head. The thought of handling any animal left me petrified. I prayed every evening nothing would visit my cage. It worked! On the third and last morning, there was still nothing. I was ecstatic, but the tutor was annoyed. I was the only student who did not have a visitation. The power of prayer, eh! To this day, I am not too keen on picking up small wild animals!

I did a teaching practice each year, but getting a school to take you was terribly difficult. I successfully asked to go to the Margaret Roper in Purley for my third practice. It was a very friendly school, and I really enjoyed it.

Headlong into my final year at Maria Grey College in Twickenham, the work increased considerably. Katherine and Alison were at St Francis RC Primary in Caterham. They were both settled into a routine, and Margaret Mace would collect them on the days I worked late at college and let them play with her kids. She was very kind, going above and beyond the call of duty to help me through my teacher training.

Margaret had moved to Burntwood Lane by this time. A big house with a big garden on a massive hill. She had no money to do it up, so it was a kid's paradise, nothing to damage or wreck.

Coming towards the end of the year, my tutor suggested I ask Margaret Roper if I could do my final teaching practice (T.P.) there. This was for eight weeks. Usually, it was frowned upon to go to the same school more than once. When I questioned my tutor about this, he said.

"I think they like you there. If a vacancy arises, they might also offer you a job."

In the middle of my final year, we were given the breakdown of what our Drama practical would involve. We had to act out a scene from a play and do a project showing skills that could be taken into the classroom. We were told we would be expected to work with our colleagues in our drama group. Everyone seemed to be getting organised, except for me. I decided to get proactive and put some feelers out about what I could do. I joined forces with Wendy Anstead and a bloke called Edward Brown. We looked around and found a Harold Pinter play, 'Beloved'. Two women and a man, a perfect arrangement for us three. I had been introduced to Pinter by Howard. Before I met him, he was into amateur dramatics and participated in Pinter's first amateur production of the Birthday Party.

The first problem I encountered was the play required some singing. As anybody who knows me, singing is not my forte. Understatement of the century: I just cannot sing. I worked hard with the song, getting help from all quarters, but with little improvement. I was so nervous but managed to get through the music. My examiner said the acting made up for the singing. Phew!

Now, to the part of the practical skills exam. Wendy and I wanted to work together rather than in a large group. It would be easier to show off what we could do. She had an old camper van, and a few of us took off to Warwick for a weekend to plan. We talked and talked about what we could do. Wendy was keen to do something with puppetry, but I was not. Puppets did not float my boat at the time. She was far more practical and hands-on than I was. We made a list of our individual skills and decided I would write a play suitable to be performed by puppets with contrasting characters. I was on a roll when I came up with the idea of placing all the saints in a factory. St. Peter was the managing director, suited and booted, St. Jude became the floor manager, and St. Bridget was the cook who fed all the factory workers. Angel Gabriel was St Peter's secretary, and St Joseph, the union organiser, represented the workers. We built a theatre, and instead of being traditional black, we made it ecclesiastical purple. Wendy and I worked with the puppets, giving them all different voices. It was hilarious and nothing like any of the other groups in the class, which I feel helped us a great deal. We both got top marks, and I learned so much on so many levels.

Throughout my teaching, I often saw the power of puppets when working with children. Through this medium, kids could often share their emotions and feelings, both positive and negative.

I am writing this during the lockdown of 2020, and my friend Heather is into appliqué embroidery. She was asked to make a family of dolls with underwear suitable to be used in child-centred therapy. The effect of the lockdown on us all had been widespread, but none more than on children. The power of puppets, dolls and toys is still poignant forty years after my ecclesiastical adventures.

After four years of serious work and commitment, I passed my exams and received my Certificate in Primary school education. Thrilled with my achievement, I started looking and applying for jobs. However, in 1977, there was precious little in the way of work. My first educational interview at Hillcrest Primary School in Caterham on the Hill was an experience to behold.

There were five other candidates in the same waiting room. Nobody spoke to each other, and you were called in individually for the interview. I sat patiently and waited and waited. Evidently, it was a long process, but eventually, the door opened, and a name was called. A person stood up and left the room. A moment later, the remainder stood up and proceeded to go!

"Where are you all going? I enquired.

"Home", they chorused.

"Why," says I.

The response was immediate.

"Because the person who was called got the job."

In suspended disbelief, I made my way to the car. I felt it was the nearest thing to a Miss World contest. I was dejected and so disappointed. There was no feedback whatsoever. What a cruel system, I thought.

Money was very tight. I was desperate to reach a stage where I didn't need to worry about bills.; I needed to earn some decent money, but no teaching job came up in my area. Undaunted, I applied for a two-week summer job teaching English to Japanese students in the church hall at John the Baptist in Purley. I got the job and turned up on Monday morning. Sixteen Japanese teenage boys sat in front of me. They had very little English, and there were no resources whatsoever. It was near chaos for a very long two hours. In the evening, I got a plan in place. I found all of Katherine and Alison's early reading and story books, plus loads of felt tip pens and got them ready for the morning. Each subsequent day, I would bring in a new everyday object, like a saucepan, cup, plate, cutlery, lamp, etc. It was a huge success. As the days went by, I started to enjoy it. It gave me a lot of confidence, but lo and behold, I got a phone call in the middle of the second week. It was from Mr Fleming, the headmaster at Margaret Roper school, offering me a full-time teaching post for September 1977.

It was a colossal relief all around, and I didn't even have to have an interview. Mr. Flemming said he had seen enough of me in my two teaching practices. No more scrabbling around looking for extra work. We had a great summer as a family, knowing, at long last, I would have a decent salary. My four years of study and hard graft had paid off. Thank you, God.

.

CHAPTER 6

Job relationships

Howard had a lot of jobs throughout his career. He was out of work when we married but got another job quickly, which was his way. We went through tough times money-wise, but we somehow always pulled through. A bank overdraft saw us through many a month. You could not call us extravagant, but we both smoked. Smoking has always been expensive pro rata to salaries.

One Saturday morning, before I became a teacher, we received a letter from the bank saying we were way beyond our limit and would have to sort it out immediately. Howard was working, and my only contribution was my Avon money. We had a long chat about what we could do, and Howard said he could give up smoking. Pigs will fly, I thought to myself. At the time, he was probably on forty a day. I must say I was very sceptical and lacked faith in the solution. He was to prove me very wrong and did give them up from Monday morning.

From that day onwards, he never put another fag in his mouth. Very occasionally, he had a small cheroot, just to be sociable. Amazingly, this made a massive difference to our budget. However, it was not the same with his drinking.

For most of his life, Howard worked in London. Taking the train every day. He worked in advertising in all sorts of guises. He had a small network of friends who were massive drinkers.

Looking back now, it seems ridiculous, but I didn't realise how alcohol played such a big part in his working life. We did not drink at home except when we were entertaining. Yes, we both had plenty on these occasions but never drank in the week.

My friend, Janet from college, was married to Paul, who worked for the Inland Revenue in Holborn. Paul became a big drinking buddy of Howard's. Colin Dunn, who used to do a lot of artwork for Howard's company, was another. He was a fantastic artist who worked with Howard for years. Roger Hurrell was another he met along the way. We were friendly with them throughout all the years. Paul and Roger both got divorced along the way. Paul was first, but I ensured we stayed friendly with all parties.

Janet, Paul's first wife and my mate, and then Gill, Paul's second wife. It was the same with Roger. We never knew his first wife but embraced Mog, his second. In each case, we never took sides.

Teaching is what I would call a very sober occupation. There is no such thing as a boozy lunch or going to the pub after work. It was the same case in all three schools where I taught. In fact, in my whole teaching career of twenty-seven years, I only ever had two hangovers. Hangovers and teaching do NOT go hand in hand.

CHAPTER 7

Irish holidays with the kids

From very early on, I took Katherine and Alison to Ireland for the annual two weeks. We took this trip religiously until the kids were in their teens. Usually, we were based at 128 Phibsborough Road. My Da's shop was at the other end of the block.

Three generations outside Da's shop

Camp Guy, another favourite location, was a mobile home in Donabate, twelve miles from Dublin. This was bought by Mam and Da, Therese and Nellie. Nellie adored caravans and was delighted to be part owner of Camp Guy. We spent a lot of time there. There is a very spacious beach within about ten minutes of the caravan. We would set off in the morning with buckets, spades, picnic rugs, towels, and enough assorted paraphernalia to ensure we covered every eventuality. In those days, cars could drive on the beach, which seems strange now. Of course, once there, we were all on foot, and everything had to be carried. At one end of the beach was a series of rock pools, and the kids would spend hours and hours messing about in the water, having the most magical of times. Therese and I would sit and natter and be delighted the kids were so happy.

Outside Camo Guy Caravan 1979

Da and Mam outside the caravan

Da in the caravan on a rare visit in 1981

Back at the caravan, mainly when the weather was not too good, which was frequent, the kids would put on concerts. Nellie had made all the kids tent-like towels for getting dressed after swimming.

One rainy, wet afternoon, they all dressed in tent towels and wrote a song called Going to Barbados. They went to the fruit bowl, took two pieces each, and shoved them in to make boobs. Anne Marie was tiny, and I remember Therese saying to her.

"Here, take a couple of plums for a small set."

We all laughed, and over the years, it was frequently reenacted.

We also played cards and board games and had lots of good old-fashioned fun. It cemented the Flynns and the Pyes together during this time.

The Pye's and the Flynn's 1979

I loved spending time there with my sister and her kids. Camp Guy provided a safe, happy place, although the site had very little going for it. There was a small, grotty shop and the most disgusting clubhouse. Calling it a clubhouse was a total insult to the word. However, we didn't stay on the site too much. We would go for walks and to the beach. When we returned to the site, we would stay inside the caravan, unaware of the outside surroundings. They were very happy times.

The botanic gardens are about a twenty-minute walk from the house on Phibsborough Road. It was another ideal trip with the kids, with plenty of green space to explore. There is only a few years difference between Katherine and Therese's Jenny. I remember Katherine's fascination with Jenny when she was just learning to walk. One day, I sat under a tree in the Botanical Gardens while Katherine guided Jenny in the walking department. Jenny was wearing a mob cap with elastic around the edge and her curls tumbling out.

Over the years, when Granny Byrne spent less time in the shop, she spent more time with the kids. On the other hand, Granddad Byrne spent most of his waking hours working, never contemplating cutting back or slowing down. After lunch, both grandparents often had an afternoon nap in their chairs. There was snoring galore. We would call them power naps now.

Da was in the shop until well after 10:00 p.m. when the shop closed. Then, the days' takings had to be balanced. If they were even a couple of quid out, he would have you there until it balanced. When the kids were in bed, I felt obliged to help, but not always. We had a telephone which went from the shop to the house. Katherine and Alison thought this was great fun and loved making calls for whatever reason.

Da was ahead of himself and the rest of the world in the technology department. He was always into the next big fad. God only knows what he would have made of mobile phones and the internet. However, I know he would have been keen to try them all out. Da also had a C.B. radio. You had to have a name to use. He was called Group Captain and would be on his radio as soon as the workday finished. It was like a modern-day chat room. All you could hear was,

"Captain here, over."

I remember one evening, a girl came on. She had forgotten to buy formula milk and did not have enough for her baby. Like the Good Samaritan he was, Da managed to find some and get it to her. He would never see anybody go short.

Alison has always been creative right from a young age. When she was seven or eight, I went to the shop for something. Da greeted me with,

"Just come and see this."

The Deli counter was usually a bit thrown together. Alison had asked Da if she could organise it for him. She had made it look fresh, tasty, and inviting. Fancy-cut tomatoes had made the whole display come alive.

"That child will go far," he said.

I've never forgotten it, but I think she has!

Katherine was the eldest of the grandchildren, followed by Paul, Therese's eldest child. Then Aileen, closely followed by Alison. Fionuala Watkins, a very close family friend from our secondary school days, had two kids, Ruth, and Naomi, who came after Alison. Then came Therese's two youngest, Jenny and Anne Marie. Every holiday as the years went by, we always had a couple of outings with the three families: Pye, Flynn, and the Watkins. Fionuala and her family lived in Clontarf, near various beaches, so we tended to be out for the day. Of course, always with a picnic in hand.

St Anne's Park in Clontarf was another favourite haunt. Many happy hours were spent exploring, climbing, rock pooling, and various other pursuits for the children. At the same time, the Mammies happily chatted away, secure in the knowledge the kids were safe and having a good time. Camp Guy was a godsend, and we were there a lot. Therese was so good to us, always cooking away and providing yummy food and treats galore. She always seemed to remember everyone's favourite.

Gertie, who was severely disabled and in a wheelchair, was a distant cousin of my father. He struck up a friendship with her relatively late in life and started to take her to Mass on a Sunday evening.

At a later stage, she began to cut his hair. It was a slow-burning relationship,

Mam used to play cards with Gertie's crowd. Cards were a huge part of family life in Ireland, although my Da never played. Over the years, Katherine, Alison, and I would visit her. My kids loved these visits as she had two fully operational wheelchairs at the back. The kids were allowed full access to them and liked to play races up and down the rear garden. Gertie was huge fun. She and I would sit with a cup of tea, watching the kids roaring with laughter. They were rough, but thankfully, the wheelchairs were quite tough. Fortunately, they only had a few minor scrapes over the years. It was a real highlight and yet such simple fun.

Mam would take us into town and buy us clothes on every trip. She had a good friend who worked in Brown Thomas on Grafton Street.

Brown Thomas Grafton Street Dublin 1974

Funnily enough, she was also called Gertie but was not related.

Mam's friend could get a staff discount. Mam loved this, just like me! Brown Thomas was the Harrods of Dublin, and my Mam loved shopping there but felt it was a bit out of her league without the discount. We had some very posh outfits over the years. She would take us to a restaurant for tea or ice-creams, which proved popular with us all. Spending quality time with Gran Byrne, as she was known to the kids, was very special.

Nellie was so good to us while we were staying in Phibsborough. Every meal was provided, and we never had to wash a cup. She was always good-humoured with a story to tell. The kids loved her. She had a friendly dog, Shane, who also gave us a lot of pleasure. The kids would love to hang around the shop and help when they got old enough.

Alison and Nellie at Phisborough Road 1984

My Mam was a great storyteller. She and Nellie played cards several times a week in various houses and would regale the goings on at breakfast. One morning, she reported something unusual had occurred the previous evening. She had been offered a grave for sale in Glasnevin Cemetery. Indeed, in those days, most people were buried in Ireland. Today, there is cremation, but burials are still the preferred way to depart. We were intrigued by this announcement and wished her to expand on the details. Katherine, who was into Irish history, asked about the grave's whereabouts. It turned out to be near the gate and right in the lie of Daniel O'Connell's grave. Once known as the Liberator, he was the Lord Mayor of Dublin during the seventeen hundreds. His monument dominates its surroundings. Buy it, they said, and then we will pray for you when we come to the cemetery. All very healthy, I felt, but the grave was expensive, and there was a lot to think about. Another factor was it was for six people, which the kids pointed out was good value. It was a hilarious chat at the breakfast table, but that is how it was in those days.

A couple of months later, my parents bought it. I visit it whenever I go back to Dublin and sit down for a chat. It brings me back to my roots.

By then, my brother Colman was living in France, and we did not see him much. Michael, my middle brother, was studying science at U.C.D. He was at college for many years while completing his Ph. D., and I used to think of him as an eternal student.

I always felt close to Michael. This was cemented when we spent two weeks together in Paris in the summer of 1963. I was nineteen, and he was fifteen. It was quite a memorable holiday. We asked Madame Camuset, the lady of the French family where I had been the Au Pair if we could stay at her Parisian apartment. They always went to the South of France in August for two months. She said yes and left us a cook who made our meals whilst we were there. Incredible really.

We had a whale of a time. Michael and I visited all the famous sites plus many art galleries. We were introduced to Max Ernst, the painter, who was fascinating. He was more unusual as an artist than other, more conventional ones. I would like to think it started our appreciation of all things cultural. To be fair, we still enjoy a broad taste in the arts.

My youngest brother Gerard had a bedroom in front of 128 Phisborough Road and never left home. Not for college, work, or anything.

During his middle to late twenties, Gerard was supposed to work in the shop but never seemed to emerge from his bedroom until near lunchtime. I think it was a bonus when he appeared. Shall we say he was not what you would call the reliable type?

Don't get me wrong, when he did work, he was terrific and knew what was required.

He was also fun-loving and always a bit of a joker, allowing Katherine and Alison a fair bit of leeway in the shop if he was on duty.

Alison with Uncle Gerard 1984

For the two weeks I was in Dublin, life just ticked over. I wanted to see everybody do everything and have a good time, but I tried not to get too embroiled in the nitty gritty of their way of doing things.

Looking back on our Irish Holidays, I tried to give Katherine and Alison a fun, child-friendly experience while having a break myself. Both were very good kids, and I can never remember them having difficulty going to bed or eating what was put in front of them. Of course, the shop was a huge novelty for them. They couldn't get enough of it. When it was suitable, they were allowed to do many things independently. I would not be chomping at the bit to join them. As a kid, I had too much shop work and saw it only as hard work and pure drudgery.

CHAPTER 8

Holidays in England

Our first holiday in England was with Howard's parents in a caravan. They booked a caravan in Swanage, Dorset. Katherine was seventeen months old and uttered her first words from her pushchair.

"Sea, sea!"

I remember the moment with utter joy. We all muddled in together for the week. It worked out alright, but we never returned with the in-laws again.

In June 1972, Maureen, our next-door neighbour, asked me if we would go to Cornwall with them to share the costs. Straight away, I said.

"Yes."

In those days, we never bothered about minor details, such as if we would all fit in the car. Will we all get on? How will the kids fare on a long journey? Just as well. Otherwise, we wouldn't have done half as much as we did.

Off we went to Cornwall. The holiday house, booked by Maureen, was just outside Newquay. Apart from being remote, the wooden structure was very damp. Katherine was three and a half, and Alison was not yet one. Of course, holiday money was limited, and I had to spend a lot on a hot water bottle to dry the beds.

Every morning, we would head for the beach with endless bits of equipment to keep the kids and adults entertained. The first morning was hilarious. Howard set off on a route march to the furthest end of the beach to be as far away from other folks as possible. Whereas Ron, Maureen's husband, parked himself a couple hundred yards from the car park.

"What are you doing?" asked Howard, to which Ron replied,

"I like to be equidistant from the chipper and the gent's lav."

Howard's face was a picture. Maureen and I just laughed as we walked down the beach to set up camp. Howard and Ron were so different and never very pally, but I have to say they tolerated each other. My attitude was we were having a holiday, and I was seeing Cornwall, so let's get on with it.

Maureen and Ron were very organised and liked to have their meal at 6.00 p.m. each evening. It meant we were all done and dusted by around 7:00 p.m. The three kids, Katherine, Paul, and Alison, would be in bed and sorted by 7:30 p.m. I don't remember any problems in that department. Maureen and Ron were not interested in going out in the evenings. They were usually in bed by 9:00 p.m., but occasionally, they would volunteer to babysit, allowing us to explore and have various little adventures. We found a local boozer, which was about two miles away. As I recall, the pub was not particularly pretty, but it was an outing. We did this several times during the week and were very grateful to Maureen and Ron for the freedom.

Howard has always been somebody who didn't like to return home via the same route when walking. I went entirely along with it. One evening, having taken a new path with little street lighting and only a small torch supplied by Maureen and the moon's light to guide us, we walked and walked. Passing a gasometer we had not seen before, we knew we had a problem. We had to retrace our steps, and all I could think of was the headline in the paper the next day,

"Couple abandon two children on holiday with friends".

We did not return to the holiday shack until 2:20 a.m. It was scary. Needless to say, we stayed in for the rest of the week and read our books!!

Previously, Maureen had been on holiday with a few different people, and they had a rule. Each family would do everything for twenty-four hours (breakfast, lunch, and dinner plus all the washing up, etc.), so you could relax and not feel you should be helping when it was not your turn. Initially, I thought it was a balmy idea, but I went along with it. Actually, it was fabulous and made it much more of a holiday. You felt you didn't have to do chores every day. All in all, it was quite an experience. I learned a lot and used this system with our friends Jean and Colin when we went on a holiday together years later.

When we arrived home, the electricity had been cut off. We were behind with our bill. I remember exactly how much we were in arrears, £9 5s 4p. I got a knot in the pit of my stomach as I searched around for a candle. The benefits of the holiday soon flew out the window. I quickly realised I needed to be able to warm up Alison's bottle. I found an extension lead and ran it out to the entrance hall, where there were plugs for the cleaners. It got us through a sticky patch that evening!!

I prayed. What was I going to do? Lo and behold, we got a £5 postal order from my Mam as a wedding anniversary present the following day. I wondered if the Electricity Company would take a down payment and promptly rang them up. Sure enough, they said they would accept anything. I legged it up to the offices in Caterham and handed over my Mam's most welcome and generous gift. After that, I always prioritised 'lecky', and we have never been cut off since then, thank God.

Howard's mother had a friend (whom we never met) who had a holiday house in Norfolk. She announced one day, we were welcome to use the cottage. It was situated near Fakenham in a place called Little Snoring. How quaint, I thought, and how English. I had never been to Norfolk and was very interested as I had dealt with Fakenham a lot while working at Smedley's. One of their canning factories was situated there.

We arrived in Little Snoring after quite a long journey. The girls were super excited to explore the house whilst Howard and I unpacked the car, which was stuffed to the gills. The house was shabby chic. It was comfy but nothing you would worry about too much, so the kids could racket around as much as they liked. It was ideal for them. We went two years running, so it gave us plenty of opportunities to explore and get to know Norfolk. The kids were six and eight the first time we went and were more independent. We usually took a picnic out for the day and went on various adventures. We visited a bird sanctuary at Blakeney with mudflats—something I had never experienced before. The mudflats were tricky, but the kids loved them, and we returned there a few times. Howard has always been keen on birds, so he would spend ages watching them, with me reading my book and the kids sinking, splashing, and playing in the mud. Perfect!

Sisterly love 1974

Family fun 1977

Norfolk 1977

Our introduction to National Trust properties was the Blickling Estate on a rainy day, which I recall was not popular with Katherine and Alison. However, Burnham Market was delightful, and I still remember the market square. It was quite unlike anything you would ever see in Ireland. Norfolk has a little special place in my heart. It is so flat and full of surprises with amazing church steeples and spires.

A huge departure for us as a family was when we went on our first all-inclusive two-week break in Devon. Mike Totterdell, whom I had worked with in Margaret Roper, recommended it. It was in Oakhampton, Devon. The owners, Mr and Mrs Friend, took in paying guests. All the meals were provided, and no washing up. Bliss. I thought all my chickens had hatched at once. Alison was eight, and Katherine was ten. The girls had their own bedroom, and Howard and I had ours. It was a bungalow with a huge front garden. Masses of marigolds growing everywhere, joyous.

Katherine and Alison, Devon 1981

Mrs Friend was a kind and friendly woman but looked quite old. In fact, she was probably no more than sixty. Her husband hovered in the background doing the 'helping' jobs with Mrs. Friend very much in charge. The food was all homemade, and we looked forward to every meal. Mrs. Friend served while her husband Edwin cleared away. One evening, she shouted out:

"Edwin, whatever are you doing?"

We all wanted to laugh but tried to be polite and pretend we didn't hear! Over the years, this catchphrase became a household favourite.

We visited the Oakhampton County show, and I was stunned by its diversity. Cake making and tasting, livestock, country crafts of all descriptions, beer tent, and afternoon tea. We had a very happy day there. In the evening, we watched T.V. (we were the only people staying), and the Friends never joined us in the front room. To my horror, when it was time for bed, I saw a large round damp mark on the wallpaper that Alison had lent against with wet hair. I was totally confused, wondering what, on earth, we were going to do. When Mrs. Friend came in with coffee, I prayed she would not look toward the damp patch! I was on tenterhooks all evening thinking, OMG, what will happen? Howard was very laid back and kept saying it would dry out. The kids were non-plussed. I never slept a wink and couldn't wait to get down for breakfast to check on the situation. The mark had shrunk to about a third of its original size but was still noticeable. There was nothing to do but to fess up to Mrs Friend.

"Oh, don't you worry, dear. We are going to wallpaper again soon." She said in her broad Devon accent. What a gem of a woman. Great holiday.

We spent days on Dartmoor, not a soul in sight. The sound of shotguns echoed in the far distance while Katherine and Alison messed about in little streams. Totally a kid's paradise. Howard and I lay on the grass, read, and slept while the kids played. Basically, we all had a whale of a time.

Howard met a bloke called John through work who lived in Coulsdon. Over time, we became friendly with the family. The wife was called Jan, and their child was named Katie. She was aged between Katherine and Alison. They owned a house in Lyme Regis right down on the front. A pink cottage, one of a pair with a thatched roof, a real picture postcard. They invited us down for the weekend. OMG, I was so excited. Alison was about three and just needed a nappy at night. Disposable ones were just coming into vogue and cost an arm and a leg. They were bulky and awkward, with a thick gauze to keep the wadding together. Horrible, really. They also fell apart quite quickly. The labels stated they were fully flushable. Yes, you've guessed it. I put them down the loo and promptly blocked up the whole system. It turned out they were not on mains drainage and had a septic tank. Fortunately, it was near the end of the break!! Still, we left with a bit of a bitter taste, giving them a lot of horrible stuff to deal with. Fortunately, we stayed friendly with them for years.

I was intrigued to know how they had acquired this cottage and, of course, a bit envious. It turned out Jan's father was Italian and was an ice cream maker. He invented the square ice cream cone and made an absolute fortune. Simple idea, eh!

When I learned this, it took me back to my childhood when I would serve ice cream through a small hatch in the window of our shop on Phibsborough Road. We never had any shaped cones, just flat wafers, which were 2d, 4d, or 6d. On a fine day, we sold blocks. A good little earner, probably!

My friend Hannah, whom I met in the library in Whyteleafe, had a sweet tiny cottage in Ightham, Kent. Initially, she invited me down with the girls. We would have a delicious lunch. She was so generous in sharing what she had with others. Everything was homemade. So much so Katherine and Alison's nickname for her was Homemade Hannah.

Several years after I met Hannah, she invested in a second-hand mobile home. It was planted at the end of her garden, tucked away in the corner. It wasn't visible from the house, which was perfect. Of course, she offered it to friends and family for holidays, and we jumped at the chance to stay. On one of these trips, we took Paul Rumbold. Like many others, his mum, Maureen, worked during the school holidays. Lucky for me, being a teacher, I got the holidays off, so childcare was not an issue.

Off we went to Ightham. Compared to our regular non-Irish holidays, it was a very short journey. In fact, it felt like it was just down the road. The kids loved the caravan; there was plenty of room to racket around, making dens, firing cushions at each other, etc. Fortunately, it was far enough from the house not to cause any bother. Also, the caravan was not exactly in pristine condition, which was all to the good. The weather, however, was atrocious for the week. I remember spending a lot of time in the local swimming pool and the Kent pubs, which sometimes had an old-fashioned games room. It enabled the kids to play skittles, darts, and even shove half-penny. It was a real treat for everyone. We had a drink, and the kids had fun and, more importantly, stayed dry.

There were also plenty of crisps to go around. In those days, kids were not allowed into pubs, and the game rooms were usually in another part of the building, away from the main lounge.

Katherine, Alison, and Paul had plenty of room to play in Hannah's garden, which they loved. She invited us to the house en famille one evening for dinner, which was very kind of her. Kids always loved Homemade Hannah's offerings. She was very good and did not crowd us during the week. We were totally free to come and go as we pleased. All in all, a nice little break.

Howard and I decided we should try a camping holiday. Colwyn Bay, North Wales, was to be our destination. We went to a camping shop in Coulsdon and hired a tent. Basic, indeed, with not too many frills, but something which would meet all our needs.

Alison was still in nappies, which is relevant to this holiday. Arriving at the campsite, we were shown to our field and picked our spot. Unpacking the tent, we realised neither of us had ever put one up this size. It was windy and cold, which didn't help. We were like cows with a handbag! Not a brass clue. Another family arrived, and hey presto, their tent was up within minutes, and they all sat down to have a drink. In the meantime, Howard and I continued to grapple with the situation. One of us had to keep an eye on the kids. It was an easier task than putting up the ruddy tent. Eventually, after a long time and much swearing and gnashing of teeth, we got the darn thing up.

I reckon it was an ex-army number and looked quite industrial. We didn't care; it was up, and that is all that mattered. As ever, the weather was not kind to us, and it rained and rained and rained. We didn't even have The National Trust to fall back on. Katherine and Alison were still too small for any such activity. We braved the beach and visited many places, but there was so little to do in the rain. Returning to the tent on the third day, we found it waterlogged. Alison's clean terry towelling nappies and a packet of bacon were floating across the floor. We both agreed the situation was hopeless and we should head home the next day.

Reluctantly, we set off, and en route, we came across a holiday park boasting log cabins. We both looked at each other and decided to venture in. When we explained our plight, the owner greeted us like a long-lost family and offered us a special price for two nights. It was out in the middle of nowhere. The nearest town was Worcester, but fortunately, they had a café. It was done out with a Wild West theme and only sold burgers, but we didn't care; it was dry and warm, and the kids were more than happy. As a bonus, we had dry beds to sleep on. The following day, we woke up to the sound of pitter-patter on the wooden roof of our log cabin. Again, we looked at each other and decided we could not face another day of our so-called holiday in the pouring rain. The woman was kind and refunded us for the second night, and we headed back to Whyteleafe. The rest of the week was bright sunshine at home, and we made the most of what was left of the holiday. We had to put the tent up again on the grounds outside the flat as it was damp and smelly. The second time was marginally easier than the first.

When the girls got to the stage where they needed more adventure, we decided to go on another camping holiday, but this time, in France.

The big difference here was the tent would already be erected, and the weather would probably be much better than our past experience.

We chose Key Camps because they offered a two-site holiday. We set off by ferry from Dover to Calais to hit our first stay at a campsite in the environs of Paris. Howard was a great driver and was equally at home on either side of the channel. Going around the périphérique ring road was a little hairy, but I think it was more down to my map reading than his driving. It was joyous to find our tent with everything in situ. All equipment for basic cooking was in place without the hassle of scrambling around eternally looking for things, which was the norm on our previous camping trip.

I was very excited to be back in Paris. Several years had passed since I had made my field trip during my teacher training. Off we set, and naturally, we were planning to do EVERYTHING as you do when you visit a city. It was sweltering, such bliss. I had fun showing Howard, Katherine, and Alison my old haunts. We ate out in little bistros, and I remember thinking we had come a long way from sharing the caravan in Swanage with Howard's parents. However, the moment was lost as we approached the Eiffel Tower along the Champs-Élysées and Katherine moaned.

" Do we have to do this?

Sunny days, Marie with the kids

Ironically, a couple of years later, when she went inter-railing with Lizzie, she went above and beyond to visit as many quirky places as possible. Secretly, I was pleased we took the kids to foreign lands. In the end, I feel it paid off. Oh, I forgot to mention that we also had Jane Cutbill with us on this trip. Her parents, Alan and Jenny, had been involved in a horrific car accident, which left Jenny poorly. Jane was one of Alison's best friends, and we felt she could do with a break. She was a smashing kid and no bother to have as an extra. It was also a good diversion for the kids.

The next leg of this particular holiday was to take ourselves down to the Southwest of France near La Rochelle. Our campsite was on the coast with lovely beaches and perfect woodland walks. The tent was spacious, with an outside living area. As far as I was concerned, it made camping luxurious. It was a large site with a kid's area offering many different activities. Katherine, Alison, and Jane could wake up in the morning and be occupied and entertained for as long as they wanted. Some days, Howard and I would go off for lunch and a long walk. Many tiny little French bistros were dotted about with absolutely delicious simple French food at very reasonable prices. The weather was hot and balmy, which made it even more enjoyable. It was a completely different experience from our soggy Welsh trip. It renewed our faith in camping and gave us such a feeling of freedom. We did some sightseeing as you do, but we were happy staying near the Jean de Pain site. It was a fantastic holiday, and we had wonderful experiences.

Returning to the ferry, I thought Howard was tired, so I offered to do my stint. I put on my driving shoes and gloves and sat behind the wheel. I drove less than 500 yards and landed in someone's driveway, which wasn't exactly the plan. Unfortunately, Howard had to take back the wheel almost immediately—poor bloke. We got to Calais in good time for the ferry, and all in all, it was a great holiday.

CHAPTER 9

Howard's passport

Over the years, Howard had some excellent jobs in advertising. While we were in Whyteleafe, he worked for a firm that did a lot of business with Phillips, which had an office in Eindhoven, Holland.

Howard went to The Netherlands to visit them on a couple of day trips. In those days, you could travel on a day pass and did not need a passport. However, his boss suggested he acquire one, as the visits would likely become more frequent. It would make life easier.

Howard took himself up to Petty France to acquire his birth certificate. An essential part of applying for a passport. However, they could not find his records. The office told him that as he was adopted, he would need to know his birth mother's surname. Howard came home empty-handed and rang his mother to get the details. She would not tell him and insisted he did not need to know anything about his birth parents as he was legally adopted. He insisted he did, and they ended up having a massive argy bargee on the phone. After about twenty minutes, Doreen shouted,

"Your mother's name was Kennedy, and she was Irish. Your father was Welsh", and then she slammed the phone down. Since then, nothing was ever mentioned or discussed about his birth or how he landed up with the Pyes. We still know precious little, as his mother would never reveal further details.

The next day, I went to Petty France with Howard. His mother was correct! Howard had been looking in the wrong section, and his birth certificate was readily available.

I remember thinking how strange it was not to have a passport and how there was a veil of secrecy over him and his position within the family. It was a big deal for us.

Having secured the passport, he began to travel increasingly with his jobs.

Howard had always known he was adopted. He got a scholarship to choir school and was a boarder from age eight. This meant there were probably few opportunities for cosy chats about his origins.

We later discovered Howard's adopted mother, Doreen, had a boy who died when he was just six weeks old. Shortly after this, she adopted Howard. Weirdly, the other child was also called Howard. Howard's adopted father was away in Wales, working for the war effort. It was 1941, and although there is no doubt he was legally adopted, there was always a veil of mystery over his background. He never tried to trace where he came from. I had several chats with him about this. The reason was he did not want to upset his adoptive parents.

At one point, the girls were keen to learn more, but their enthusiasm never came to anything. I was very ambivalent about the situation. It could have unearthed a happy saga or a whole can of worms. While I was not totally against investigating further, I understood why Howard was happy to leave things as they were.

Howard's parents were born in the early part of the 20th century. It was an era where family secrets were never openly discussed.

As far as I know, following the harrowing telephone conversation with his mother, his adoption was never mentioned again in his parent's lifetime.

CHAPTER 10

Early work

Whilst at home with Katherine and Alison, I continued my Avon business. This was convenient as I could go on my rounds with the kids in tow. Not only was it social, but I could earn a few bob with every bit of profit going straight into Lloyd's bank. All the cashiers knew I was saving for the deposit for a car, and I got a great kick out of seeing my money grow.

Area meetings were held in the Blue Anchor in Croydon, where I would meet other reps. I became friendly with the area manager, Mary, and discovered she was also Catholic, which was bonding. She became a kind of an auntie figure to me. I did my Avon round for a long time and became quite adept at making it work. Every month, prizes were awarded for target sales. I have always loved an incentive and still have a set of wooden table mats, which have done sterling work for the past fifty years.

The part-time Smedley's working arrangement with Maureen ceased two weeks before Alison was born. There was no such thing as maternity leave, and I longed to do something constructive. Opportunities were thin on the ground with two small children.

However, my social network expanded, and I enjoyed life. Katherine and Alison were good kids, but they grew and developed fast. I joined a dressmaking class in Adult Education in Caterham. I was hopeless at sewing, but Nellie used to help me make dresses. I was probably suffering from a false sense of security. The spec in the brochure said to buy a piece of material and pattern for the first session. So off I went and purchased a piece of woollen cloth and a Vogue pattern.

I rocked up to my first class, and the tutor said to me,

"Oh good, an experienced dressmaker."

"No, quite the reverse. "I said.

She looked me straight in the eye and shouted,

"Well, why on earth did you go for a Vogue pattern?"

I felt a pattern was a pattern. I was arrogant and didn't give a stuff, thinking I'd manage. Of course, I found dressmaking excruciatingly difficult, and even though I failed to complete the task in the term, I embraced the whole experience. Naturally, in the end, I took the unfinished garment home to good old Nellie in Dublin, and she finished it off for me. Thank you, Nellie, champion woman.

I made lots of pals throughout my time in the sewing class and broadened my friendship group around Caterham. I am still friendly with Margaret Bushell forty-seven years later. It was not a disaster, even though dressmaking was not in my D.N.A.

The Pye sisters - 1973

CHAPTER 11

My first job at Margaret Roper

Margaret Roper was a well-established Catholic school sharing grounds with Thomas More Senior School in Purley. Mr Fleming placed me in Year 5 (or old Junior 3). It was full of ten-year-olds, so once you are organised and know what you teach, you are in business. I felt I was more suited to the older children. Having done two teaching practices at the school helped immensely. I was familiar with the staff, surroundings, layout, and routines. Mike Totterdell had started as the Deputy at the same time. He used to come into my class to do maths support. This was very welcome, with thirty-five children in my class and a wide range of abilities.

I was looking forward to half term, but lo and behold, Mr Fleming called me to his office (a rare occurrence). He announced he was putting me into the Reception Class after the break. The blood drained from my face, and my brain said, "Holy shit", how will I transition with only six weeks of actual teaching under my belt. Planting a false smile on my face, I made no protest. The reception teacher was moving up North with her husband, so it was a fait accompli. Leaving the office, I formulated a plan. After school, I collared Dee Ramsay, the reception teacher and begged her to help me, before she left. She had been there forever and was very experienced. Dee generously gave me two days in the half-term round at her house and taught me apparently silly but essential things like how to get each child to know where to hang their coat, etc. I got a small notebook and wrote down songs, ideas and almost everything she said. I worked hard to succeed in my first year in Reception. The younger the age group, the more challenging the teaching. I was enthusiastic and loved teaching and all it entailed. Of course, that helped. I also found the trick with small kids was to be well-prepared and keep them focused and happy.

Howard's father, Bertie, suggested over Christmas lunch, I move Katherine and Alison to Margaret Roper. As far as I was concerned, they were happy and thriving in St. Frances in Caterham. Initially, I thought he was cuckoo. However, Howard and I discussed it in great depth, looking at the advantages and disadvantages. There were other staff with children at school, and it seemed to work for them, so we decided to go with it. However, the one thing we didn't consider was whether there would be places for them. There wasn't! Mr Fleming said he was very sorry, but his hands were tied as he had no vacancies in years one and four.

"No worries, I will get on to the Holy Spirit, and he will sort it," I said.

He roared with laughter.

Lo and behold, a few weeks later, a family moved to Bermuda, and, as we say, the rest is history. Happy Days!!

Howard and I took the girls to the front room and laid down the ground rules. They were to ignore the fact their mum was a teacher at their school, and they were never to visit the staffroom pestering me. Throughout their primary days, I was amazed at how they coped and gave me no concern. It was terrific for me to have them there on so many levels. Good man, Bertie, you were far-seeing.

Mike Totterdell was keen on cross-country running and introduced it as an after-school club. I had no idea how this worked or the rules, but I was willing to help. Howard had been a good runner in his day, and both the girls inherited his athletic genes. Katherine joined the club and showed a real aptitude for it. She was very sporty, and it came naturally to her. I helped with the club and began to learn all about cross-country running and remained enthusiastic throughout my career. Mike started The Croydon Cross Country Schools Association, involving several other Borough schools. It is a fantastic sport that enables every child to participate, regardless of ability. We had huge grounds and could host matches at our school.

Alison was also very talented and joined when she was old enough. She always came high up in the winning team. The school competition was held twice a year, but our girls needed more, so they joined Mitcham Cross Country, Howard's old running club. This meant training every Tuesday and Thursday evening plus Sunday morning. Their headquarters were in Carshalton. Howard and I shared taking them to training, and then, joy of joy, we started sharing with the Woodleys. They were another family whose daughter Karen was also a handy runner. This was a massive help, as three times a week was a big commitment. Mitcham was uninterested in you unless you turned up consistently three times a week. I would park under a lamp post near the club and use the light to do my marking. It was a great training workout for the kids, giving them exercise and keeping them out of mischief (not totally, I might add!). Cross country was a new world to me as I was not the slightest bit sporty. The scoring after a match was a lengthy job (before computers), which I loathed, but Katherine and Alison were particularly helpful until the novelty wore off!

We took the kids to matches all over the place. With well over a couple hundred in each race, Katherine and Alison were challenged and had to fight hard to stay near the top of the leaderboards. It got us to places we would never have ventured to as a family and was great fun if a little on the muddy side. It was a good foundation for both girls. Even though they are now in their fifties, they are still active in the sport. A good return for all the ferrying about.

Mike Totterdell left Margaret Roper quite suddenly after a few years. He got a headship in Sutton and left at Easter. Consequently, I inherited some of his responsibilities, one being Cross Country. The season's final match was to be run at Margaret Roper on a weekday after school. It was my first inter-school match without Mike. After teaching all day, I got ready to receive about ten other schools with their runners, parents, and teachers. As they began to arrive, the weather turned quite nasty. Cross country is run rain or shine, so I honestly wasn't bothered. We went ahead. Thunder and Lightning decided to pay us a visit at the end of the first race. Mumblings went all around the grounds.

"Are we cancelling?"

"What are we going to do?"

Unaware of the vast dangers (i.e., lightning hitting a tree), I was not overly worried and wanted to finish the match. Thank God it all went off without a hitch. Looking back, I was so lucky.

Being the new teacher at Margaret Roper, I had all sorts of responsibilities. There was little movement of teachers, which meant folk were quite stuck in their ways. Being the new kid on the block and enthusiastic, I was happy to embrace new opportunities, including collecting the tea money! Some teachers were somewhat reluctant to pay up weekly. However, I had a child in my class called Raquel. I felt she could do with some extra responsibility and put her in charge of collecting the funds for tea, coffee, milk, biscuits, etc. She was very persistent and would not leave until she had money. It started to show a profit early on, and I have always been very grateful to her. She taught me a good lesson about how to delegate.

A few years in, Miss Jones, who ran the netball team, decided to move. Katherine and Alison were more than handy at Netball, and when I heard the news, I realised there would be no Netball club. I felt so sorry for all the kids. I popped into Mr Fleming's office and asked if I could take it over. Sitting back in his chair, he announced, "Certainly". Nothing more. He never enquired what netball experience I had. By the way, it was nonexistent! That afternoon, I stopped in Purley and bought an easy guide to Netball, and my new career began.

You actually do not need to be an expert to teach Netball successfully. The girls worked hard, and I did my best to give them fun and motivate them. I organised the teams and took them to away matches for about five years. Later, I took an adult umpiring course. I was aiming to improve my skills. I loved it and played a bit myself. Being tall was my only attribute, so naturally, I was placed in the goalkeeper (GK) position. You haven't got to move too much! Playing with Katherine and Alison was fun, as they were exceptional in their positions, making life much easier for me. Thank you, girls. I didn't realise it would stand me in good stead in my career. In my last year, the children's parents gave me a bespoke paperweight to mark our success. I was chuffed to nuts and felt very proud of myself.

Another thing I inherited from Mike's departure was a school journey to Wales. I had been to Guernsey as a helper the previous year, so I had a bit of a clue. However, the Welsh trip was activity-based. The teacher-parent helpers were terrific. They all pitched in, but I was the leader! Health and Safety were an extremely low priority in those days, which gave rise to a hairy situation during a horse-riding session. Around thirty kids plus eight adults bowled up to Farmer Giles, who equipped everybody with a horse but no helmets. With no practice whatsoever, off we trotted. It was my first time on a horse, and I would guess it was the same for most of the party. Alison was with us on this trip. It must have been difficult for her to have had a mother everywhere during primary school. You did so well, Alison! Having your mother in charge was not an easy gig.

The horses were quite docile, and the session went fine until the end. The horses stampeded as we returned to the farmyard, and two children fell off their mounts. It was a pure miracle everyone walked away completely unscathed. I have got to say thank you, God. A couple of hours later, it dawned on what could have happened. The severity of the incident came crashing down upon my shoulders like a ton of bricks. It was an enormous responsibility. From that moment, I put safety very high on my list of priorities. This applied to all my further adventures.

Christmas has always been one of the year's highlights in our house. I was legendary for spring cleaning for Santa! One year, in early December, our last one in Whyteleafe, I came home from school to find a large upright freezer outside the front door. A note on it said,

"With love from Santa".

"What," I said,

I could not work out where it came from. We certainly had no money to purchase a freezer. My

Mam had sent money to Granny Pye, who organised it and arranged for it to be delivered from Allders in Croydon. Mam felt it would make my life easier since I had two hungry kids and a full-time job. It certainly did change the way I shopped and cooked. It was my first year of teaching, and having a regular monthly salary was beginning to make a difference. It was so far-seeing of you, Mam. Thank you so much.

When I went home to see all my family in Ireland the following summer, my Mam told me to get a cleaner for the next academic year. I thought she was nuts and dismissed her ideas completely. Later, giving it some thought, I realised she was right and went ahead and found a lovely lady called Angie. Since then, I have always had a cleaner. They tended to stay for several years; I even helped some move into new positions. I think having a cleaner changes your life for the better. Mam, you were a wise, grounded, fun-loving person. Thank you.

Returning to Christmas, I aimed to have fun and do as little work as possible over the holidays. This was a hang-up from my childhood. As a kid, together with my siblings, we worked in the shop right up to the wire. The Christmas tree would go up on Christmas Eve, and we would be in the shop until quite late selling picture boxes of chocolates to blokes for their wives on their way home from the pub! Then, if we still had holly wreaths to sell, we would open the shop on Christmas Day for people to buy and take to the cemetery. Back in business on St. Stephen's Day, there was little time for leisure. Determined our family Christmas would be completely different. I always booked the pantomime, which I adore, for the matinee on Christmas Eve. In later years, Katherine and Alison were reluctant to come as they found me a bit of an embarrassment shouting out, "He's behind you, etc."

Home from the panto, Howard would peel and prepare the veg for the festive feast. The kids would get into their pyjamas, and we would open a box of chocolate biscuits—a rare treat in those days.

I'm thrilled 1981.

Nativity production 1981

Happy Christmas at No 76

Will it Flame 1973

One particular year, we were all watching T.V., the goodies were all laid out, and the house was sparkling. About 7.30p.m, there was a knock on the door.

"Who on earth can that be?" I said to myself.

I opened the hall door, and there was Father Christmas in person on the doorstep.

"Who are you?" I shouted.

Father Christmas," he declared.

I was like a jabbering idiot, but I let him in. He said.

"I hear you always spring clean for Santa, and I have come to inspect your kitchen cupboard."

Then, as he opened the kitchen doors, the so-and-so said,

"They are not as good as last year!"

I didn't handle it very well, saying.

"Who are you? WHO ARE YOU?"

He talked to Katherine, Alison, and Howard, and they were thrilled. He never once dropped his guard and left after about twenty minutes. We never knew who it was until several weeks later.

It turned out he was Jeff's best friend in the cricket club. His children were grown up, but he still loved dressing up as Father Christmas. Jeff told him how nuts I was about the man in red, and as we say, the rest is history. It certainly made our Christmas.

When we moved to Purley Park Road, the kids could walk home from school together. Initially slightly worried, I soon relaxed and was delighted to give them some independence.

Over my time at Margaret Roper, I did Reception plus Years Five and Six. When Alison reached Year Five, I was going to be her teacher. Not ideal, but Mr Fleming did not mind. It had happened with other staff members, so it was not an issue.

Again, I laid down the ground rules, but Alison had her own request, which was very specific. Howard was to book a proper father's appointment for Open Evenings. She also insisted it should not be the last appointment. The reason was Alison wanted us to discuss her progress properly. It was to be an appointment in the middle of the session. This would enable Howard to come home and take her to the front room as we usually did and talk about her progress. We adhered to her wishes, and I was delighted she took it so seriously. We also had a strict rule that whatever happened in the classroom with her would stay there. I tried to be as fair as possible but didn't give her any concessions!! Her class was lively and kept me on my metal all year. Alison worked hard, and it was a real privilege to have had the experience. Both Katherine and Alison had lots of friends in school. Going to pal's houses was a treat, while cross country and netball took up a chunk of the week.

As Margaret Roper had a swimming pool, I took the opportunity to take my swimming teacher's certificate. It was one of the hardest pieces of paper I ever had to work for.

There were two parts: practical and teaching. Learning to dive for a brick and swimming in my pyjamas were challenging! Katherine was my guinea pig for my teaching practice. I prayed to be given backstroke in the exam. It was the easiest, as you can see the child's face. It was, and I passed!!

It was very handy when Alison had a swimming party for her ninth birthday. They all jumped in excitedly, and I acted as the lifeguard from the side. As I watched, I noticed one girl sink straight to the bottom of the pool. Instantly, I jumped in fully clothed and hauled her up. It turned out the girl couldn't swim! Fortunately, after a bit of coughing and spluttering, she was fine, thank God. I asked her why she jumped in. She said she thought she would be okay as everyone else had done it—the joys of being a teacher! We went on to have a fun time. Hurrah.

During my time at Margaret Roper, Katherine moved to Coloma Secondary. I wanted the girls to attend a Catholic School, and Coloma had an excellent reputation. However, there was no guarantee she would get a place. We looked at the various options but felt Coloma was the best by a country mile. The day dawned for the interview. Howard, Katherine, and I went in to see Sr. Mary Cuthbert, the headmistress. She quizzed us as a family. Then Katherine was whizzed off and cross-questioned by two people in two separate rooms. They wanted to know if she was a real live catholic! Meanwhile, our interview with the brave Sister was pretty innocuous, so I said in a loud, begging voice as we stood up to leave.

"We are desperate for her to come here."

As we walked to the car park, Howard said.

"Well, you have blown that!"

The point he did not get was I was trying to ensure she remembered us! Thank God it seemed to work, as Katherine was accepted.

That same Christmas, my Da sent us a turkey through the post! It was plucked but needed cleaning and hanging. I had seen thousands of chickens and turkeys go through their paces at Phibsborough Road. However, I had never cleaned one. I don't remember setting out to avoid doing this work. I just wasn't very good at it. Therese, in particular, Colman and Gerard were much better. Michael and I were in the same boat. Lucky us.

So here I was with this bird needing to be cleaned and the sinews pulled. We had a special hook in the shop for doing the sinews but no such item in our flat. I phoned Da and got instructions on doing it over the top of the door. We managed it, and I was delighted to hear a crack indicating the sinews had broken.

When we moved to Purley Park Road, we invited Howard's parents for Christmas. They would stay in the spare room. How posh!! Well, the first year, they arrived, settled in and then Mother came down the stairs with a tablecloth and draped it over the television. She then placed a pot plant on top, saying we don't watch TV over Christmas. We went along with it just to keep the peace. Our new friends, the Cruwys, invited us to a Boxing Day Party the same year, but Mother and Father wouldn't go. Howard went with the kids while I stayed home with the reluctant grandparents. The following year, I set the ground rules. I'm happy to say we never had a repeat performance and enjoyed many happier Christmas days together.

As I said, Katherine transferred to Coloma in September 1980. We were thrilled she got a place but then had to work out the logistics of getting her there. Two buses were needed to make the journey. In the summer, we did a few practice runs. She had to be in at 8.20 a.m., meaning we all had to rise earlier as a household. Around this time, I changed from being a night owl to listening to the dawn chorus.

Sister Mary Sheila was a force to be reckoned with and kept the girls in order, including our Katherine. Alison followed Katherine to Coloma in 1982. It was a great relief the sibling got in. We still had to go through the interview procedure, but knowing a place was secure made it easier. She was in the first year of the new GCSE, which replaced O Levels. They were a complete unknown, with everyone in the dark. The main difference was they appeared to involve a lot of coursework. I remember going to the open evening. When I reached the English teacher's desk, she looked up and said, "Oh, marvellous news about Alison, isn't it?"

"What news?" I said.

"Oh, you know we got permission for Alison to do book coursework on Jackie Collins."

I was so annoyed they hadn't even bothered to get in touch to discuss the situation. That's how schools operated in the early eighties.

When the GCSE results were released, Alison was in hospital, having her adenoids out. She did brilliantly. Well done you.

The year Alison did her GCSEs, she was going out with Steve Court, who lived locally. The same year, Howard and I went to Devon on holiday to a small hotel for a few days, just the two of us. On the first evening, Alison phoned to say Steve's mother had arrived unexpectedly from Greece and had nowhere to stay. His parents had been divorced for years. She asked if the mum could stay at ours. Initially, it was to be just for one night. I was pretty laid back about the whole thing until we got to the third evening, and Alison announced Steve's mum was Irish, and we were bound to get on like a house on fire. I became slightly concerned as she had been separated from Steve's dad for years. We had a spare room, so I could see it becoming tricky. She was still in situ when I spoke to Alison the night before we were due to come back to Purley. I put my foot down and insisted she was gone upon our return! She was, so the situation resolved itself, thank God. I never did meet the woman, but I hope she went on to have a happy life.

By the time they were in their late teens, we had started leaving the girls alone in the house. We trusted them, and Howard and I felt it was a way to ease them into responsibility for themselves and their actions.

The flip side for us was we got to go away and have little adventures of our own. Howard and I loved spending time together and had great fun. The added bonus was the house was always far clearer when we came home than when we left. It was a win-win all round. Thank you, girls!

The Cruwys were great party throwers, but I never wanted to go to one on Christmas Eve after our Panto outing! One year, Jean begged me to come, and I agreed only if we could leave early. So off we popped to Hillbury Road, and as ever, it was buzzing chez Jean. However, I stuck to my guns. Around nine o'clock, we decided it was time to leave and go home to Santa! No food had yet been served, so Jean said to let the kids go into the dining room and help themselves before we left.

On the way home, Alison said.

"Mum, why do you never buy any of that brown meat?"

After some probing and questioning, we ascertained she was talking about smoked salmon. She had eaten all the fish, removing it from the top of all the canapés. The minute I got home, I had to ring Jean and tell her she would have to do a rescue plan as Alison had scavenged the table like a locust. Jean was so gracious about the whole business. Thank you, Jean.

The kids were desperate for a dog. I was less keen. Eventually, I gave in with firm assurances going for walks would not be a problem. The first Saturday after this, we set off en famille to the RSPCA rescue centre in Godstone. We did not go with any pre-expectations; we just wanted a dog.

We filled in a lengthy questionnaire and looked for one we liked. Each we picked out resulted in a big fat no. The RSPCA turned us down, mainly because they were not keen for the dog to be left alone all day while we were at work and school. In the end, feeling very frustrated, I said.

"Is there a dog you would actually allow us to have?"

The girl laughed and said, "Well, we have Yogi." She led us over to his quarters. He was a woolly, low-down fifty-seven variety. We took to him straight away. It turned out Yogi was nine years old. At that time, I didn't know it was old for a dog. He had been an old lady's pet. His owner died with nobody left to look after him. Yogi was a poor feeder and was pining for his previous owner. We said we would give him a go. They told us he liked cooked potato skins and we should boil them for ages before giving them to him.

"No problem", we replied, not realising what a vile job it was. I did the skins once. Yogi took a sniff and declined. I then got him a variety of dog foods to see which one he might like. Problem solved, or so I thought.

We took him to cricket on Saturday afternoon. He seemed happy enough, but he never touched a morsel the whole weekend. We were getting worried as by Sunday evening, there was no change. We always had sweets on Sunday evenings. Katherine and Alison were dispatched to the local garage for supplies. Everyone chose their favourite. This particular weekend, wine gums were on the menu. When Yogi heard the rustle of the bag, he was very interested and woofed up several sweets. From then on, we never had any more trouble with his dog food and, thankfully, not a potato skin in sight!

Besides noshing on sweets on a Sunday evening, we all spent fifteen minutes sharing the ironing. I was determined the kids would learn some household chores as they grew up. Unlike their mother, who came to most household skills quite late in the day!!

Yogi was a massive part of our family, and we loved him to bits (even me). I saw the joy the others got out of having a dog. It was a good family decision all around. As Yogi was quite old when we got him, we worried about his longevity and decided after a few years to get him a friend. Off we went, back to Godstone. This time, it was much easier as we were tried and tested. We came away with a much younger dog. Kim was three years old and a Labrador cross or a high-up dog, as I described her to my friends. They got on well together and tolerated the cats, so it was one big happy family. Walking was never a problem. Howard was particularly brilliant in that department. He got up early and took them to the Rotary Field in Purley. The kids were also pretty good.

Yogi lived to the ripe old age of fifteen, which was fantastic. We got Kim when Yogi was twelve, so they had three happy years together. Unfortunately, entirely out of the blue, Kim had a massive seizure. Fortunately for me, Katherine, who was at home, took her straight to the vet, but nothing was to be done. As both kids had left home by this time, Howard and I decided not to get another dog. We just stuck to cats.

.

CHAPTER 12

Move to Purley Park Road 1978

When we moved into our flat in Whyteleafe in 1969, it cost £4,250, and the housing market rose considerably over the years. Although we were extremely happy there, it was only a two-bedroomed place and somewhat on the small side. We knew we would move one day but were never in a rush. Also, there was the little question of having the wherewithal to go elsewhere. Prices of property were going a bit mad.

Howard's parents were vaguely thinking of moving and had their house valued. They were just about to put it on the market when the 'boys' (great friends of theirs) came round to dinner and offered them £8,000 more than the asking price. The 'boys' had always loved 'West Winds' and were keen to get their hands on it. They were traders in the City, and there was no shortage of readies. Howard's parents were amazed and grabbed the offer with both hands and promptly moved to The Tower House, a first-floor retirement flat in Cuckfield. It was an old, converted Queen Anne mansion.

Tower House Cuckfield

One Friday evening, shortly after this, Howard and I had a bottle of wine and beef burgers (high living) and began putting the world right. We discussed the sale of his parent's house and then the question of us moving. We felt the two city boys knew something about the housing market; otherwise, why would they offer so much over Howard's parents' asking price, unheard of in those days. So, we hatched a plan.

We contacted the estate agents the following morning and had the flat valued. They came back with £14,999, and we were staggered. We then looked to see what was on the market. I was still working for

Margaret Roper in Purley, so we decided it would be sensible to move that way. Also, there were better train links to London for Howard to commute to town.

There was precious little on the market. However, estate agents gave us three houses we could look at. We looked at their locations to see how we felt about the area. We wouldn't even consider one but made an appointment to view the other two. The first one we rocked up to, the door was opened by a bloke who said.

"Sorry, already sold, "and banged the door in our faces. We were shocked.

The next day, we turned up to the second on our list, Purley Park Road. Although it wasn't furnished conventionally, we loved it as soon as we crossed the threshold. The front room had a piano and masses of nude paintings (very amateur, not good) propped up against the walls, nothing else. The middle room had fireside chairs in a circle and looked like an old people's home! It had four bedrooms, a breakfast room, a kitchen, and a substantial garden.

76 Purley Park Road

We wanted it and put in an offer, which was accepted. It was February, and the owners said they didn't want to move until July. It suited us admirably. We had no idea of moving in two weeks as we had done previously. Even so, it felt like we were in a whirlwind. Five months of thinking and consolidation was precisely what we needed. It was all very exciting and gave us time to get organised.

Katherine and Alison loved the flat at 33 Hillside Road because the grounds were huge. They used to raid the rubbish area for things for their camp, e.g., a piece of carpet, an old stool, bottles, pots, and pans, etc. They made these fantastic camps. Writing this in lockdown, I never worried about germs or restricting them. They had so much fun, and I'm sure they learned many skills through their creative play. They spent hours and hours playing in these hideouts. They were the oldest kids in the flats, but by the time we left, there were eighteen others.

They would be out playing for ages, and I would ask Howard to go out and check if they were okay. Thankfully, they always were. One camp would last for weeks whilst they added to it. Then, a terrific new item, such as a piece of matting or lino, would emerge, which inspired a new camp. We always insisted they tidied everything back to the rubbish area before they started a new one.

For the first few months in Purley Park Road, they were bitterly disappointed the garden did not lend itself to making camps. I was not too sympathetic about this and felt they should be delighted to have a super garden of their own to use. I realise it was perhaps mean of me, but they found their way after a while.

The new house had quite a big rear garden, which backed onto a railway line. We inherited a large pear tree (great for a swing) and a cute small pond with a low wall.

Alison under the pear tree 1979

There was not much in the garden but buttercups and daisies. The kids really missed the vast expanse of the community gardens in Whyteleafe.

Over the years, Howard transformed the garden beyond all measure. It turned out he had a natural talent for gardening.

With plenty of room at the side of the house, we installed a netball post. Swingball also became a firm favourite.

Relaxing in the Garden 1996

Slowly but surely, the kids started to have their own fun. When Wimbledon was on, tennis was popular. We still talk about Tracy Austin, and I remember them asking if they could have green towels to be more like Tracy. I laughed! No chance! Howard was very sporty, unlike me. The girls got a lot of their skills from their dad, and occasionally, he would play in the garden with them. Another favourite of theirs was a golf course constructed with jam jars. In fact, in the end, the garden ended up as a massive success and a virtual extension of the house. The kids always brought their friends around, and whatever was in the fridge would be shared. Sunday lunch would often run over into the late afternoon.

With its dinky little wall, the pond made the perfect place to sit and chat. It was ideal for our legendary gatherings and family meetings. On one occasion, when the kids were starting puberty, I took each of them there and gave them the infamous sex education talk. Reminding them to make sure they use a condom! Not very catholic at the time, but nevertheless, the chats went down in family folklore.

Over the years, everyone was welcome, and I encouraged the kids to have their friends come round and was thrilled to have them sleep over. Mind you, only weekends and holidays, not any old time. I preferred to know where they were; it seemed to work over the years.

I remember one funny incident when I got up one morning, and a teenage lad ran down the stairs in red underpants and asked me,

"Do you live here?

"Yes," I said, pointing out we only had one bathroom, and I would get priority. Strangely, I am still in touch with the chap!

The Croydon girls ready to hit the town in 1991.

I loved living at 76 Purley Park Road. It was a lovely family house. After our two-bedroomed flat in Whyteleafe, it was so roomy. We also had a spare room with plenty of space. It had a square bay window, which gave the room a quirky shape. The house was Edwardian and very solid.

We always had cats right from when the kids were small. We used to call Howard the cat lover from Surrey. Whilst we were in Hillside Road, he arrived home from work one evening with a tiny, scrawny black kitten. A litter had been born near his office, and this was the last one left, the runt. I can take animals one way or the other. When I was growing up in Ireland, we always had cats. It was essential, I think, to control the mouse and rat populations. Ours were kept outside and fed off scraps. There was not too much pampering going on. Once, when I was about eight years old, I remember my Da cornering a rat with a yard broom and wringing his neck. It was horrible, and I don't think my father was in any way delighted with the experience either. Fortunately, I only remember it happening once, so I think the cats did their job.

Katherine christened this little cat Pickle. He went on to live to a ripe old age and was much loved by us, even me! While we were in Whyteleafe, I seem to remember another cat called Millie. She was a little devil for peeing on the carpet and always in one place. I tried everything under the sun to get rid of the smell, to no avail. Ultimately, I had to cut out a particular section of the carpet. It was so impregnated with wee it had rotted. She was not one of my favourites!

We had three cats when we moved to Purley Park Road. Somebody said they should be the last to be packed into their cages on a moving day. Also, upon arrival in the new house, they should be put in a room for a few days with all their gear to get used to their new surroundings. This was good advice, and I would probably not have been so diligent if left to my own devices. We would bring them out in the afternoons or evenings when we could give them love and attention. They settled in beautifully, and we had no trouble with them.

Our last two cats were a brother and a sister. We seemed to have difficulty finding names for these two. I couldn't deal with their nameless status, which had lasted a few days. Off to school one morning, I said to Howard,

"Please have names for those two by the time I return this evening."

I fell about when he told me he had chosen William and Mary. My immediate reaction was, how could you go into the garden and call out those names? Looking back, I was quite up myself.

CHAPTER 13

Cricket in my DNA

As more and more children were born on Hillside Road, the parents' social life improved considerably. On a coffee morning, I met a girl whose husband played cricket for Queen Mary's Hospital in Carshalton. She waxed lyrical about how family-friendly the club was and how they were looking for new members. It sounded idyllic compared to the club in Caterham, where Howard played the odd game. She inquired as to what positions he played. I was still ignorant about the rudiments of the game, and all I could say was he was an opening batsman and a wicketkeeper. The club jumped at having him. We had no car then, and a girl called Freddie used to transport us everywhere. Three kids, four adults, and the cricket gear piled into the car and off we would go. The club was very child-friendly, and the kids made many pals. Before long, I was on the tea rota but never reached the high echelons of keeping score.

Freddies's gang at the Sunday Times Fun Run 1981

We went every Saturday throughout the summer and made many friends over the years. The kids played on the sidelines and watched. It was also the start of Katherine's cricket career, culminating in her playing several matches for England. Unfortunately, women's cricket had not gotten off the ground then and still had a long way to go to get the recognition it deserved. Another factor was when she was at the Body Shop, she had to work Saturdays, making weekend sport a serious no-no.

The game slowly grew on me, and I decided it was time to visit Lords, the home of county cricket. Freddie and I took the kids to see a test match. Howard, who had never been, could not join us but was delighted I was going. We remedied this years later and went several times together. Cricket has been a huge part of our lives; it has given us lots of pleasure and a common interest.

As I entered the gates of Lord's Cricket Ground, I didn't really know what to expect. Having spent many hours watching club cricket, making tea and learning the game's rudiments, I was at its home. Finding our way to our seats, I was uber-excited.

The first ball left the bowler's hand and spun through the air, and I watched avidly as it made its way towards the bat. No run. The hush in the crowd was palpable. As the bowler ran up, he released his second delivery, and again, the ball ascended towards the batsman. Connection, smack, he hit it for four. The crowd were ecstatic. Silence as the third ball was hurled through the air. Thunder was heard in the distance, and the heavens erupted, followed by a rapid exodus off the pitch.

There was nothing for it but to have our picnic early. As the rain fell in torrents, we went to the cider tent. Everyone was merry, especially after a couple of pints. Although marginally bothered by the lack of cricket, they all seemed resigned that not many more overs would be played. However, I was determined to enjoy my first test match regardless. I went off to explore the grounds by myself. Well-equipped, I donned my bright red raincoat with a matching sou'wester hat and braved the elements.

Setting off in a clockwise direction, I came across the merchandising shop. Huge; I couldn't believe you could buy so much gear. The prices were sky-high, and I wondered if they were in league with

Harrods. As I continued, I noticed a pavilion with chaps standing all suited and booted. Seeing how formally they were dressed, I realised each wore a tie. Oh, I thought, who needs to be so stuffily dressed at a sporting venue? I reported my findings to my friend Freddie, who informed me the pavilion was strictly men-only, with a particular smart dress code. I was shocked and found it somewhat hilarious and old-fashioned, even for 1977. They were all standing on the terraces, drink in hand, waiting for the cricket to resume. Hatching a plan, I said, "Let's gate crash it."

"Impossible," she said.

"Let's try it," I said.

"We can go over the low wall in the front and keep moving towards the exit at the top of the stand. We will take a drink from one of the trays on the way. I bet not one of those stuff shirts will say a word. They will be so gobsmacked they will do nothing."

She was game, so taking a deep breath, we set off. It went totally like clockwork. The look on the old boys' faces was priceless. If only I had a video.

CHAPTER 14

Dinner parties

Dinner Parties were a big part of our lives in the '70s and '80s. Restaurants were very much for special occasions. There was no such thing as having dinner out without a particular reason. Mind you, the same could be said for lunches, even coffee. A cup of tea may be in the afternoon, but it certainly was not the norm as it has become today.

Our first dinner party was for Howard's Mother and Father, Doreen and Bertie, to announce I was pregnant with Alison. I did Devilled Kidneys, which I loved. Also, as there was not a lot of money sloshing around, it was a relatively cheap option. Kidneys were very much included in our diet in Ireland, and I did them with sherry! I thought it was très posh. Unfortunately, Mother was not too keen, but she did eat them. I then discovered offal was not popular in Britain. Back in Dublin, the liver, kidneys, and the occasional heart were normal for us as kids, and I always found them very tasty. Needless to say, Howard's parents were delighted about the pregnancy.

We did entertain a bit in Whyteleafe. I remember Margaret Mace and Bobby came to dinner; the other guests were our friends Wendy and Brian. Margaret got upset about something, probably to do with too much Guinness and locked herself in the loo. She never appeared for the rest of the evening. Funnily enough, Margaret only ever came to dinner one other time in our friendship, and again, there was an issue centred around drink. She made life quite tricky for the rest of us. After the second incident, which was quite a time after the first one, I decided that was it. I never had her to dinner again. This did not harm our friendship and never became an issue between us. As far as I was concerned, she had more than enough other qualities to compensate.

Katherine and Alison were terrific in helping at these events, particularly when we moved to Purley Park Road. They would serve the starter and be really brilliant. I relied on them a lot. They would set the table and do lots of different jobs. Thank you, girls. You made a huge difference, making my life much easier and more fun. Anti-pasta, cold salami, olives, etc., were a big favourite. I would try something new and then have it a lot. Most things were made from scratch, and I tried to make everything as tasty as possible. Lots of wine flowed throughout, which helped the ambience and atmosphere. Brilliant conversations and discussions were usually the order of the evening. We were renowned for good fun, honesty and, of course, good craic.

I think Katherine and Alison also liked these evenings as they would get to go and watch television upstairs with goodies galore and were allowed to stay up late. I look back on those times with such fond and happy memories. Now I realise that by giving the kids a bit of slack, they grow and learn. Howard was always very good with the clearing-up.

Your friends form a big part of your life, and I now know how much I have learned from them. They broaden your horizons, views, and ideas, and then you can make up your mind and form opinions or even change your beliefs. Nothing is set in tablets of stone. Following a particularly lively evening, I would reflect on the session's content, sift it all through, and decide what was good or bad. I tried hard not to be judgmental and took the attitude to live, let live, feeling blest to have folk around the house.

It was fun putting people from different parts of the forest together. I love hearing about people's lives, mainly when they differ from mine.

I still feel like this today. I had an excellent lecturer at college who gave a talk one evening about learning throughout life. I thought it odd at the time, but now I know differently.

Howard and I were known far and wide for our St Patrick's Day parties. They were legendary. Our friend, Colin Dunne, would create the invitations.

I remember the first time we hosted the world and his mother: mums, Dads, Children, and even the odd dog. I remember feeding all the kids in our tiny kitchen in No 33, and although I enjoyed the party, it was a lot of hard work, and I felt there must be an easier way.

We put our heads together with the Dunns for the next one and devised a theme.

It was the Olympic year 1990, and the invitation was about participating. So, we had Conditions of entry: 1 bottle, 1 Irish Joke and 0 children. It worked a treat. We gave everyone plenty of time to find babysitters—a win-win situation.

SELECTION MEETING
FOR THE
IRISH TEAM FOR THE
1990 COMMONWEALTH
GAMES
will take place on Sunday
18th March 1990

Special Events
Hop, skip and try to stand up
Clay Pigeon Shooting with real
clays
The Marathon – anyone still
on their feet by 7.30pm
stands a good chance of
winning.

Conditions of Entry
1 Bottle of Booze, no kids.
1 Irish joke

Starting Time
12 noon

RSVP to
Team Manager
Marie Pye
76 Purley
Park Road
Purley
Surrey
CR2 8BT

1990 Commonwealth Games Party Invitation

Our friends started to get to know each other, and we had great fun. We would begin at lunchtime, and they would go on well into the evening. I made Auntie Gerry's ball curry a lot. The batch was a bit hot, but plenty of water was available. At the next party, I was ultra-careful not to make the same mistake and reduced the heat. Strangely, a couple of chaps said.

"Oh, Marie, it is not as good as last time."

Hilarious. It reached the point that if I served anything differently, I was sure somebody would complain.

It is incredible how vogues come and go; dinner parties were undoubtedly a huge part of most people's lives in the late 70s and 80s. Certainly, the ones we knew.

I wonder if they will make a big comeback following the COVID-19 epidemic.

Who knows?

CHAPTER 15

St Chad's Primary School

I spent seven happy years teaching at Margaret Roper Primary School in Purley. During this period, there was a dearth of jobs, and only a couple of other opportunities arose that I was qualified to apply for. The first was at Courtwood School in Selsdon. I didn't get it! The second was at St. Chad's catholic primary school in South Norwood. In this case, my application was successful. The post was in charge of maths. I had just completed a two-year diploma at Wimbledon College, and with a promotion in mind, I decided to take the opportunity. It worked!

However, the school was trashed and vandalised three days before the first day of term. Doors were ripped off classrooms, and every bit of new stationary and stock was rendered entirely useless. The perpetrators had taken all the tins of powder paint and sprinkled it everywhere. They had really gone to town in their destruction. Miss Betchetti, the headmistress, called all the staff in for a major clean-up. I remember removing sacks of debris off the floor of my new classroom. It was touch and go if we could open for the start of the new term. However, with all the staff working together, we were successful.

What a baptism of fire. My classroom did not have a door for months, which initially was disconcerting. Eventually, when it was re-hung, I liked the open-door arrangement so much that I never closed my classroom door for the rest of my career. It was very cathartic and transparent, so good.

It was a small school in quite a deprived area, but the kids were delightful. I learnt a lot from Miss Betchetti and the rest of the staff. She was old school and totally child-centred. To her, problems didn't exist. They were only challenges to be solved. I found some staff reluctant to change and very set in their ways. Quite a learning curve, I would say.

We didn't have morning playtime outdoors. Instead, the children had the entire run of the classroom and shared areas with indoor toys. The kids got the gear out and put it away. Remarkable. They had been trained in the Reception class to do this. Her idea was with outdoor play, there would be ructions without adequate supervision, whereas the indoor sessions were very civilised.

As is my wont, I thought some of her philosophies were balmy, but upon reflection, I realised her systems worked well. This was my first step into management, and I tried to learn every step of the way.

She played classical music during assembly while the children wandered in and sat anywhere. There was no regimented lining up, and their behaviour was admirable. It was very forward-thinking and ahead of its time.

While the indoor morning playtime was good for the children, the staff had to grab a quick coffee, wee in relays, and organise supervision. However, kids did go outside at lunchtime, when the dinner ladies took over and did a splendid job.

There was a tradition of shared lunches. Once every half term, a list would go up, and you would write down your contribution. These were jolly affairs, even without wine. (You had to teach in the afternoon.) I remember quite a bit of a one-up-manship regarding the contributions and the innovations. I went with the flow and didn't get involved in the politics.

During my time at St. Chad's, Katherine and Alison were still in Coloma. Occasionally, they would come in the car with me as I could easily swing past their school. Mainly, they went independently on the bus. It was also a time when they were both preparing for exams.

Katherine and Alison had a secure set of friends, thank God. This was hugely important to me, and I encouraged them to see their friends outside school. They were also into their sports; we still ferried them here and there and everywhere. I suppose it was all part of parenting!

Before her final year, Katherine went on a holiday to Wales with her mates. It was her first independent holiday away from us. Upon her return, she announced she was gay!

At first, Howard and I did a fair job trying to persuade her she wasn't. A natural first reaction. This continued for about six weeks until Howard and I sat down and had a frank and honest discussion. We realised in our hearts it was evident our daughter was gay, and we should just accept it. We all chatted in the front room, told her we were totally on board, and supported her all the way. As a family, we never had any problems with the situation. However, I cannot say the same for others. Well done, Kathrine, for handling it all so well.

Sometime later, Howard's mother, Granny Pye, came round for Sunday lunch. While sipping her sherry, and out of the blue, she asked us if Katherine was gay. After we said yes, she said she had known for a while, and it was good Katherine had come out so early. While we took it all in our stride, we were delighted Granny Pye was so modern about the whole subject. She was well-informed as she had had 'the boys' as great friends for years.

Doreen was a remarkable lady for her age and asked for a subscription to the magazine Vogue for her 90th birthday! That says everything.

Alison did her GCSEs during my final year, and Katherine completed her A Levels. She was hell-bent on going to Liverpool but unfortunately did not get the grades needed. At this point, I didn't know it was the Irish capital of the UK.

Our school secretary, Imelda, said her husband Vincent tutored A-level English.

"Great," says I

She also informed me her husband didn't take just anyone. They had to be serious about getting their required grade. He sent a message to say he would interview Katherine. OMG, I felt a pit in my stomach. This was serious stuff.

Katherine never wore anything but trousers, apart from her school uniform, which both the girls loathed. However, I insisted she wear a skirt for this ordeal. Seems so ridiculous now, but somehow Katherine conformed. Thank you, Katherine.

I never met the famous Vincent and sat in the car during the interview. When Katherine returned, she was ashen but confirmed he would take her on. She was allowed Christmas Day off, while every other day would be a study day!

The retake was in February, and she passed with flying colours. In the meantime, we had no money to send her to Crammer College. We also felt we couldn't let her slosh about for the year, leaving her to her own devices, so I investigated Croydon College. It didn't have an excellent reputation then, but it offered a course for an A-level in one year. Katherine took history.

Her tutor rang me about two weeks into the course. Katherine was not getting on too well, and her attendance was dodgy. I said I would have words with her and sort her out. His response was unexpected.

"No, Mrs. Pye, I don't want you to say a word to Katherine. Just tell me a bit about her and what makes her tick."

I duly filled him in, and he thanked me for my honesty and assured me if things didn't improve, he would ring me in two weeks. Under no circumstances was I to tell Katherine about the phone call. I kept my word. There was no call from him, and Katherine passed her exam at the end of the year. He never rang again, and Katherine headed off to Liverpool in September.

Alison was fourteen when I went to St. Chad's and was ensconced in Coloma. She had lots of friends and enjoyed the social side. It was the first year of the GCSE exams, which replaced O levels.

Homework 1984

Ready for school 1985

She had a boyfriend, Steve Court, and was in the hospital, having her adenoids out when the results came through. She did exceedingly well, and we were all overjoyed, so she went to the 6th form. Early one afternoon in October, I came home from school and was greeted with the following:

"Mum, I need to talk to you."

She did not want to continue in school. I somehow knew that having a massive argument with her would be futile. We sat down, talked it through rationally, and devised a plan. It was a Tuesday, and I told her she could leave school if she had a job by Friday. Alison's initial concern was what I would say to the school about her absence. I reassured her that I would say she had a bad cold. However, if she succeeded in getting a job, I would inform them she was leaving.

"But I haven't got a cold," she declared.

"I think a little white lie is in order in this instance," I replied.

Alison looked surprised:

"What, you would tell a lie? OMG, I used to think you were so honest."

I was pleased my principles had rubbed off on her.

By the end of the week, she got a job in Hertz car rentals. It only lasted a few months, but fair play to her, like Katherine, she realised that she needed more qualifications and embarked on a commercial course at Croydon College.

I prayed she would be offered the job when she went for her first job interview. She was, but she didn't take it!! Alison was incensed she would be expected to work in a basement with no window. Initially, I felt she should have taken the job. However, it was a different world in 1987. I was proud she was her own person even then. Alison quickly secured an alternative position with Office Angels. It was an excellent experience, and she matured a lot.

A short time later, Alison and her friend Claudia decided they would like to work for Virgin Atlantic as trolley dollies. After some research, they discovered the interview process would be over a couple of days and using a calculator for sales was a high priority. The girls swotted up and got themselves fully prepared.

Unfortunately, Claudia agreed to dye her hair the night before, and the process went horribly wrong. She emerged looking rather orange. Not daunted, they dolled themselves up, but poor Claudia didn't get through to the second day. However, Alison was successful and worked as an air hostess for several years. Alison was always excellent at networking, and when she felt she needed a change, she took a job at Virgin Bride—a one-stop bridal service, which, in its day, was an innovative concept.

Then, when Richard Branson started Virgin Mobile, Alison joined them on the ground floor. She worked there for many years before going to Australia in 2005.

Katherine worked at the Body Shop as a Saturday girl before she went to Liverpool University. After her degree, she returned to the Body Shop and joined them in a managerial position. Katherine remained with them for several years before moving to Neil's Yard. As a political animal with a small p, Katherine loved ethics and philosophy, which was very avant-garde in the late eighties.

Both my girls had various relationships over the years. I would hear about some escapades but let them get on with things. On the other hand, my two brothers, Colman and Gerard, had difficulties from their teenage years. This resulted in my developing a mantra for my kids. Be happy and learn a living. I realise it was a tall ask, but I was keen they did not go down their uncle's route. Howard and I loved living at 76 Purley Park Road without kids. They came home frequently. Sunday lunch with their Pye parents was a regular feature. I knew vaguely what they were up to but was happy not to know too much.

The three years I spent at St Chad's were very educational. Miss Betchitti was a very unorthodox headmistress. I learned an awful lot from her. She put the children bang in the heart of all her thinking. She firmly believed EVERY child deserved umpteen opportunities and recognised they sometimes had enormous hurdles to climb.

It was vertical grouping, which meant you had children from two age groups. I took years four and five, so you would have the children for two years.

One of these children was called Boris. He was a challenging child from an interesting background. Boris had three brothers, all with the same mother but different fathers. Boris was taken to see his father's grave every Sunday, whereas his brothers spent the day with their respective Dads. Monday mornings were tricky, to say the least. Miss Betchitti would say,

"Remember, Boris doesn't have to start the day with Maths or English. Let him be creative."

It was a great idea but not so practical as many other children would love to join Boris. By the time I had had him for two years, I had done my best but was ready to hand him to the next teacher in year six.

When I returned for the new term in September, the brave Boris was still on my register: shock and horror. I marched to the Head's office and demanded to know why. It seemed she felt I was so good with Boris, and he was so happy with me that Boris should continue in my class. I tried to stand my ground as I felt very hard done by. The Head did a deal with me. When Boris cut up rough, I was to take him to her office. Poor Boris was gone within a week. I often think of him and sincerely hope he is having a good life.

Another lad used to eat pencils, literally. It was terrible for his digestive system, not to mention my limited supply of pencils. After a long search without the internet, I found liquorice wood, which he chewed instead. Problem solved.

It was a caring, nurturing school and an excellent place to prepare for my next move.

CHAPTER 16

Move to Oak Lodge

I had kept in touch with Mike Totterdell since our days at Margaret Roper, where we worked together, and I helped with the cross-country. In 1988, while chatting to him during a match, he mentioned he had a senior job available at Oak Lodge School, where he was the Head. It was a large primary school in West Wickham. For me, it would mean a massive jump from 150 to 630 children. However, I felt I was ready for the challenge on many levels. Katherine and Alison needed me less and less, certainly physically. As their Mum, I always tried to be available for them emotionally when they needed my support. But I also wanted them to become independent young women making their own stamp on the world.

I was ecstatic when I got the job, but of course, quite apprehensive at the same time. Before

145

term started, I held my first management meeting with my team, which consisted of a husband and wife plus three other teachers. Mike Totterdell, who had been in post for two terms, had followed a Headmaster who had run Oak Lodge since Adam was in the fire brigade with a long-established staff who were very set in their ways. Generally, they were not too keen on a change of any description.

At the meeting, I got quite a grilling. The first question was something along the lines of:

"What on earth qualifies you for this job, with you being Irish?"

I told them I had completed my teacher training in the UK and went on to talk for several more minutes, expanding my qualifications and experience. They were seemingly satisfied, and we had a very successful session. They were more than helpful as I navigated my way into senior management.

It was my first secular school, and I had not got the 'Jesus Factor 'to fall back on. A couple of days into my new job, a little pickle was sent to me at lunchtime for calling another child's mother a tart.

"Do you know what a tart is?"I asked.

"Of course, someone who sells their body for sex, not the Mr. Kipling variety!"

I was gobsmacked. He was such a bright cookie who taught me a big lesson and forced me to look at how to deal with discipline without the fallback of the saints. I took several courses and devised many systems, hopefully enhancing the school's ethos.

As staff, we devised a system where everyone sang from the same hymn sheet. Most important in a large establishment. I worked very hard to bring people together. After much deliberation and pooling of ideas, we came up with the motto:

Treat everyone like you would like to be treated yourself.

I worked in the Upper School all my eighteen years, bar the last year I spent in year three.

The autumn term in Primary school is probably the busiest, culminating in the Christmas Nativity contribution. The first year I arrived, I inherited the local Baptist Church in West Wickham as the venue, which had been used for years. I remember marching the whole Upper School there for our first rehearsal, all 200 kids. It was not a huge place, but the children were as high as a kite with excitement. When you are in charge, the other teachers tend to sit back and let you get on with it. So, I tried to position the children, asking them to move back towards the altar.

"We can't", they kept exclaiming.

I couldn't understand the problem and raced to the rear to see what was happening. I found the back row of children teetering on the edge of a fully immersive baptismal font. My heart missed a beat when I realised what could have happened. It was rectangular, lined with marble and empty. A lucky escape. You acknowledge the enormous responsibility of having other folk's children in your care on these occasions.

Thinking on my feet, I had to manoeuvre the kids into a different configuration to make it a safe situation for everyone. I am glad to report all the performances ran smoothly.

However, the following year, I moved the carol service to St. Marks, which was very near our school and convenient. The church is octagonal, so the wide expanse of the altar is suited to performance.

I worked with a few musical directors over the years. Apart from the odd minor hiccup, there were no major incidents except for one year. Sue Carter was new in post and slightly apprehensive about working in a catholic church.

"You will be fine", I reassured her as we set off for our first rehearsal. As ever, the children were so excited to be out of school. Sue was at the front and entered the side entrance, with kids following.

Within moments, we all came to a halt as she came racing out and over to me, whispering.

"There's a body in the church."

"Is it in a coffin, I enquired?"

"Yes, but it is in front of our performing space."

Mr Smith, the teacher from Year five, said,

"No bother, I'll get some parents to move it to the side."

"No way," says I, visualising the corpse sliding out of the coffin.!

"Well, what are we going to do?" screamed Miss Carter hysterically.

I was all for continuing as I am well used to coffins left in the church the day before burial. I called the parent helpers into a little huddle and explained the situation. The consensus was to do the rehearsal around the coffin. I told them I would explain to the children what was happening before we started.

We entered the church; Miss Carter was far from happy and promptly fainted on the floor. There was no way she could carry on. Leaving a couple of adults to deal with her, I told the children we would return to school. The poor kids, not to mention the parent helpers, were in total confusion. By this time, I was in a bit of a spin when I heard Miss Finch announce.

"I wonder what we will do when we return to school."

"I will do an assembly, talk about death and then give the children a slightly longer playtime," I announced.

I felt the children had a right to know what all the commotion was about. I told the teachers they didn't have to attend.

"This I've got to see," said the brave Miss Finch.

I somehow found the right content, which was tricky, to say the least, in a non-church school. The assembly went off without a hitch.

The headmaster sent for me at lunchtime to congratulate me on my sound decision and finished by saying,

"Imagine the headline in the Sun Newspaper. - Children dance round coffin; a new slant on the nativity story,"

Thank goodness he did not know about my earlier thought processes.

Alison had not lived at home since she was eighteen and was making her way into the world. She had various relationships, and then she met Bernard. Still very young, they decided to get married in Barbados. It was in term time, so I could not go. There was also the question of cost.

Bernard's parents were French but lived in Coulsdon. Our families jelled well, and I found it a novelty to try out my very rusty French at these gatherings. Unfortunately, the marriage only lasted a short time. It must have been a difficult decision to get divorced, something not taken lightly. Alison got on with her life in her own unique way, and I admired how she handled the situation.

Eighteen years is a long time to work in the same place, but Mike Totteldell steered the whole ship through calm and choppy waters, and I felt lucky to have such a fantastic job. I kept learning and developing, and so many experiences came my way.

I kept my home life and school life relatively separate and did not let them become merged.

I have strived to learn from my ups and downs, and when criticism (hopefully constructive) came my way, I realised it was for a purpose.

I never let the children out precisely on time. The main reason was we had a system whereby the class would tidy the classroom before they left to go home. We always seemed to run over by a couple of minutes.

One afternoon, we were five minutes late. When I came outside with my charges, one of the mothers ripped me apart for never getting out on time. She screamed and hollered, saying she was now late for her daughter's dental appointment.

I was shocked about how she went for me in the playground. It was not a regular occurrence at Oak Lodge. However, by the evening, I could see it from her perspective. The next day, ensuring the kids were out at 3:15 p.m. on the dot, I apologised to the lady in question. She told me she was going through a choppy patch in her marriage, and maybe she had been a bit harsh.

Over the next few months, I worked more closely with the family as my pupil showed signs all was not well on the home front. Initially, the mother didn't want to know, but I persevered. By the end of the year, we had a good working relationship. My one aim was for her daughter to thrive in my care.

I never ever let my class out late again, literally to the end of my school career.

Over the time I worked with the child's mother, I saw her turn herself around. Nearing the end of term, the child was leaving for Secondary school. The mother and I were on a relaxed footing, and I said to her.

"Follow your dreams."

She grinned and said, "What would yours be, Mrs Pye." Caught a little bit on the hop, I uttered.

"Mine's a hot air balloon ride to go off into the sunset."

Not thinking another thing about it, I was astounded when, on the last day of term, the class presented me with a card announcing.

- *Mrs. Pye, you are off on a balloon ride to follow your dreams-*

My trusty mother had organised a collection to make it happen.

Thank you; it was the most magical experience and something I will never forget.

My school experiences have been many and varied. Children are so spontaneous and open. They provide a rich tapestry. I feel the secret to personal development is never to stop learning. I see my mistakes and realise nobody is perfect, least of all me, and it is better to embrace what is thrown at you. The characters you meet in life are extraordinary, and I love the phrase – ***Take what you like in life and leave the rest.***

CHAPTER 17

Kids Moving on

By the time I had reached my forties, Alison had de-camped to a flat at Emma Arden's house. Meanwhile, after university, Katherine got a job in management at The Body Shop and moved back home.

She had been with us for a while when I came home from school one day to find fourteen black plastic sacks lined up along the landing. She was going through her black trousers, jumpers, and tops, stage and saying things like:

"Mum, do you like this new outfit?"

My reply was always the same. "It looks very like your previous outfit."

(Hence the number of sacks.)

Or she would say:

"Please, can I put them in Alison's room?"

"No," I said firmly.

"Well, what about the spare room?"

This time, I was even more adamant.

"NO"

"Well, I will have to move out then, "she responded.

"Go ahead," I said.

She found a bedsit within a cup of tea distance quite quickly. I was delighted as I felt it would be good for her independence. I helped her to her new flat, turfing her stuff onto the pavement, and never even gave her a hand to take them inside! It was hard, but I needed to be strong. I have often wondered how it would have panned out if I had not made a stand!

Katherine and Alison have a terrific work ethic and, thank God, have never been out of work. They became very independent young women, and I am immensely proud of them.

Howard and I bought our first caravan in 1991. It was cited in Pagham. Howard and I would go down frequently at the weekends. The girls were busy working, socialising, and having fun. Boyfriends and girlfriends came and went but were only introduced when the relationship became semi-serious.

Howard's parents would sometimes come to Sunday lunch in Purley Park Road, and the kids would turn up and be dutiful granddaughters, for which I was very grateful. His parents were so formal, and the kids were so not; the contrast between the two generations was striking.

Granny Pye with her grandchildren in 1990

One weekend, both kids stayed overnight and rolled out of bed moments before Doreen and Bertie arrived. Howard's mother uttered as they descended the stairs in torn jeans (the height of fashion at the time).

"I didn't know we were not dressing for luncheon".

"You are lucky they turned up at all", I replied crossly.

I loved the kids coming around and hearing all the latest gossip from their worlds. They were funny and put on a genuine show. Family is very important to me, and I loved these get-togethers. One or both brought a pal or two, adding an extra dimension to the table. We had legendary Sunday lunches with lots of fun where the day's issues would be discussed from every angle.

Howard had always been a heavy drinker. I never thought it was much of a problem in the early days. I was brought up in a place where people drank socially. Also, there was a massive drinking culture in the seventies and eighties at lunchtime. It was totally the norm, and nobody questioned it. Howard was out of work when we married but quickly got another job. However, he frequently lost jobs, and I never joined the dots. Why not?

I love Howard very much and forgive him a lot!

In September 1977, I qualified and received my first salary. I felt relieved and took over the finances; Howard was very happy. Less responsibility for him! He always used his credit card, whereas I preferred to pay upfront. However, it meant, on occasions, I had to clear his massive credit card bills, which took me forever. This happened twice, and I was livid. The monthly interest was eye-watering and mounted up so quickly. It is also a terrible waste of money, and you get nothing for it.

He had some great jobs over the years and managed to keep them for a decent amount of time. He wrote off a car at MEL, based in Crawley—a yellow Datsun. Not surprisingly, he was banned from driving for two years. However, he fell on his feet, and a colleague in Purley gave him a daily lift to and from work. He spent two years at MEL but was then out of work again. This fallow time lasted longer than usual, and he eventually decided to work in a factory on the Purley Way. After that, he started a gardening business. He had always been a terrific gardener but without very much technical knowledge! Two teachers from school became his first customers, and he went on to do okay. Gardening is very much a word-of-mouth occupation, and recommendations are crucial. He got the jobs, but the alcohol started to take its toll.

The crunch came for me one Saturday. I was due to take ninety-five children from school to Shropshire for an activity week and was flying around like a whirling dervish, getting everything ready. I looked out the kitchen window and saw Howard lying on the grass. I went out to investigate, and he was out cold, so I called an ambulance.

"He is drunk," they said.

I was honestly in suspended disbelief. The ambulance men were even reluctant to get him into the house.

"Give him black coffee and keep him awake", they advised as they left.

Adrenalin is a remarkable substance. It kept me going for the evening. I got up the following day, shoving Saturday's events on my back burner and hardly gave Howard a second thought for the whole week. On my return, I realised things had escalated without me noticing. When the penny finally dropped, I knew I must address the alcohol situation.

After much research, I found Al-Anon, an organisation for families and friends of alcoholics. It was a lifesaver, and I attended weekly meetings for years and years. I was a slow learner, and it took me a long time to understand you are only responsible for yourself. Slowly, over time, it began to seep in. I met several amazing people who really did understand the effects of alcoholism on each member of the family. Although everyone's alcohol journey is entirely different, it was enlightening to use the Al-anon programme and have like-minded folk to support me. I will be eternally grateful for the privilege of listening to everyone's stories. It helped me learn how to deal with the situation.

Howard was happy for me to attend, and of course, I always kept an open dialogue as to where I was going and what it was for. We continued to live and do things together.

The support network in Al-anon is phenomenal. The fact everyone in the room had been affected by the problem was very reassuring. Because alcohol is used as a social commodity, most people feel alcoholics should stop drinking and stop causing havoc in the lives of those around them.

Unfortunately, this is not the case, and it took me years and years to get the message. I am only responsible for myself, and it is up to me to change. Keep doing the same thing, and you get the same result.

Al-anon is the sister organisation to Alcoholics Anonymous (AA). I do not know where I would be today without the help, love and support I received. I did work hard, one step forward and three backwards, but somehow got to a good place where I could grapple with Howard's alcoholic escapades.

Several years later, Howard did recognise he was an alcoholic. However, I feel he accepted this in name only, making only a few feeble attempts to attend AA meetings. Although he went through all phases of the journey, he never got the message. Howard was sober for fourteen months, which was bliss, and just when I stupidly felt thank God, this is it, he returned to his old habits.

You must work hard at sobriety. It didn't continue for Howard, making life much more difficult for the family. Not knowing what was around the corner and the unpredictability of the next episode was very difficult to deal with.

Howard did go through a phase where he only drank at home. This was good for me as we could socialise with friends, and I could have a nice time. Mind you, I kept a beady eye on the situation, ensuring there was no secret vodka hidden away in the boot of the car, etc.

Over this time, his relationship with both Alison and Katherine deteriorated dramatically. They visited less frequently as he went increasingly into the depths of drunkenness. I met the kids away from home, and fortunately, I also had a lot of friends who helped. Some knew the situation, and some didn't.

Katherine and Alison were getting on with their lives. They were working away, and I would meet them in London. Katherine bought a flat in Kentish Town, while Alison bought one in Hilldrop Crescent. Alison had also moved to Virgin Mobile and was going from strength to strength. Her office was in Leicester Square, and I would meet her there from time to time. On one occasion, we went to an exhibition at the National Gallery showing the exhibits that might be on the fourth plinth in Trafalgar Square. There were six of them, and a public vote for the winner. It was in the very early days of putting different art up there. Alison and I had a special day, and I admired her stripy-coloured scarf, which she gave me. I was very moved and still have it.

When I met Katherine, she always had friends in toe. However, I was delighted to get together under any circumstances. I remember we visited the Saatchi Gallery on the Southbank one Sunday just before it burned down. I was introduced to Tracey Emin, Damian Hurst, and Grayson Perry's work. Not bad for one afternoon!

My girls have been superb through difficult times. They looked after me by involving me in their lives. For many years, they were unprepared to have Howard involved in social outings or activities because of his antics. Initially, I was upset, but as things worsened at home, I realised it was for the best. Of course, by this time, I was in Al-Anon and beginning to get the hang of the twelve-step programme.

It was not all doom and gloom in any shape or form. Howard and I continued to do things together. The caravan was a great go-to place for us. We have always loved the theatre.

Howard was a good actor in his day. He was the lead in the first amateur production of The Birthday Party when Pinter himself attended the Chipstead Players. Amsterdam was our place of choice for our 25th wedding anniversary.

Amsterdam, 25th Wedding Anniversary Cruise

We celebrated our 30th anniversary at the Edinburgh Festival. Unfortunately, this was one of our last memorable anniversary celebrations. After Edinburgh, we took a road trip to different parts of the country we were unfamiliar with. I loved it. Finding out about areas I knew nothing about. One of our favourite activities was to try and catch evensong and visit different Cathedrals.

Looking back, I always lived my life to the full. The school was all-absorbing. However, I feel I have achieved a fair degree of balance between work and home life. My friends have always been incredibly important to me. Sharing my problems where

163

appropriate was very cathartic. Teaching is so full on there is not much room for private thoughts during the day, and I got highly adept at switching off my issues that were sounding off in my personal life. Thank God for my two girls. They always listened to me when I was banging on about Howard. So many happy and fun times in our lives ended up in disaster, often when we least expected it (or maybe we were). Alcoholism is a progressive disease; in poor Howard's case, this was undoubtedly the situation. It was very much a yin and yang life. Howard had many admirable qualities and was always very supportive of all my escapades. He helped me over the years when I struggled to combine study for my Arts degree with the Open University, teaching and family life. However, I did manage to graduate. Thank you, darling.

Graduation 1995

Katherine and Alison were remarkable in how they handled both of us. I certainly was not a bundle of fun at times, and they pulled me up short occasionally. I wasn't always too receptive, but again, Al-Alon helped me to realise my shortcomings. I got a lot from taking my Fourth Step Inventory:

'Make a searching and fearless moral inventory of yourself. Then, admit to God, yourself and another human being the exact nature of your wrongs.'

Around this time, I felt I needed to apologise profusely to both of my kids for all the harm I had caused them over the years. I was in fear and trepidation as to how it would go.

My wedding anniversary was coming up. However, by this time, Howard did not attend many celebrations. Katherine and her partner Amrit lived in West Hampstead and invited Alison and me to lunch. There was a cute little garden out the back, and we were having drinks and nibbles when I broached the subject. I had brought a dose of Al-Anon literature to help me. The girls were magnificent, and we had a great discussion, which cleared the air. We could all exchange how we felt and how to look at a way forward. The outcome was we would socialise and connect with each other without involving Howard too much. I can feel the relief now and am so grateful for their honesty.

Thank you, girls.

CHAPTER 18

Escapades with Howard

(Not all doom and gloom!)

If any school holidays coincided with Howard working abroad, I grabbed the opportunity to go with him. With no kids at home, it seemed a no-brainer not to miss out on an adventure.

He went on many trips overseas. China, the United States, the Middle East, and Europe. Of course, I could not go with him on some of these. The first evening I stayed in Purley Park Road alone, I woke up at midnight and saw a light from the garage shining onto the garden. I lay in bed for ages worrying, not knowing what to do. Eventually, I gave myself a good talking to, grabbed a walking stick with a metal top (ever prepared!), and braved it outside. Relief, I had left the light on. After that episode, I was never fearful of being on my own. Being apart for short periods was very good for us; I felt it gave us a broader perspective on life. We were fundamentally good pals and tolerated each other's foibles.

A trip to Turkey coincided perfectly with my half-term. Istanbul is an awesome city full of such contrasts. Standing on the side of the Bosphorus, the sea strait between the Black Sea and the Marmara Sea (which looks like a river), I remember thinking, OMG, I am looking over at another continent, Asia. We bartered for leather coats and felt so sophisticated. However, before heading to Antalya for the rest of the week, we had great difficulty persuading a vendor outside the Blue Mosque we could not take a Turkish rug on the plane to the UK.

Istanbul is a place of contrasts. Our hotel was opulent and spacious, covered in marble, and so luxurious, but it was surrounded by poverty. Seeing the haves and the have-nots at such close quarters was dreadful. It was a salutatory lesson for me.

Singapore was another highlight for me. Stepping off the plane, I felt I was walking into a plant house in Kew Gardens. Our hotel room was a suite similar to a small apartment, and waiting on the table was the most enormous bowl of fruit imaginable. While Howard was busy working, I organised outings to nearby islands and had a fantastic time meeting all sorts of different folk. It was exciting.

Singapore1992

Rome and Paris were other destinations. Of course, every trip had twists and turns, but I loved every minute. It was great spending time with Howard and, at the same time, doing our own thing.

Howard and I have adventurous streaks but have always taken each other's suggestions on board. Despite the roller coaster journey, I will always value what we have together.

Swanking it up at the Hilton 1984

CHAPTER 19

Work in progress

When I embarked on this memoir, I thought it would be chronological. Very early on, I realised this was impossible as life goes off on many tangents, with events and memories shooting off in all directions. Soon, it became like an octopus with umpteen tentacles.

In 1993, a deputy headship came up at Oak Lodge, and I applied for it. The interview was thorough, and I felt a lot of pressure being an internal candidate. The educational boffin from the Council on the interviewing panel asked me.

"What is your definition of spirituality?"

To this day, I have no idea how I answered him. I think the Holy Spirit himself took over. I was sure I had fluffed it, but I was thrilled when I was given the appointment. Somehow, I had to go up a notch as my new job description had more elements. Howard, Katherine, and Alison were so proud and supportive of me.

As this was happening, Howard was into his gardening business. I was relieved as I was getting fed up with his yin and yang employment situation and felt there might be some chance of stability. Ever the optimist me! He had an innate talent and always knew whether something needed trimming or cutting despite having no idea what was what! He built up quite a client base. One day, he arrived home with a greenhouse. He had done a big job, and the lady said she had no money. She asked him if he would like the greenhouse as payment. I guess she didn't want it. Cheeky, but it served us well for a long time.

Howard didn't see much of the kids except when they visited for Sunday lunch with Granny Pye.

Alison was divorced from Bernard by this time and was living in her flat in Hilldrop Crescent. She was going from strength at Virgin Mobile. Katherine was working hard, living in Crystal Palace.

My philosophy was always to know if the kids were content and making their way in life. I would be happy. Looking back, this was also when I was dealing with my issues at home and Howard's drinking.

I loved my work, which was all-consuming and challenging. It provided me with stability.

My Mam had a long, slow illness which lasted for seven years. She was diagnosed with myelofibrosis (a type of leukaemia). I was very close to her, and during this time, I was going to Ireland (only during the half-terms and holidays) on my own.

She loved an outing and still had her sense of fun, and depending on her energy levels, we would go off on little sorties. I was the prodigal daughter and knew the real caring fell to Nellie, Therese, and her family.

A favourite place was the Royal Marine in Sutton on the Northside of Dublin. She was always ahead of the game. One day, she asked me to order a West Coast Cooler, a cocktail in a bottle. It had only just been launched. I admired the fact she never lost her sense of joy.

By August 1991, she was in the hospital, and I spent most days with her. As I was about to return to the UK, she said.

"Marie, can you do my nails?"

"Why?" I replied.

"Because I want to look good in the coffin."

This conversation allowed us to have a frank discussion about her dying. She really wanted to go.

She used to have her platelets changed frequently as part of her extremely draining treatment. I joked with her she should not leave her departure for too long so I could return before the start of the new term!

What a privilege to talk with my Mam on such a level of honesty. She died on the 4th of September.

In Ireland, funerals are arranged and completed usually within three days. However, in our case, Colman had to be located and come from France, and I had to travel back from London. So it took slightly longer.

I arrived at the house to a frenzy of activities. Da was making a wreath with Mam's favourite flowers. Nellie was busy in the kitchen dealing with and feeding the callers who came to offer their condolences. Therese was organising the Order of Service. However, Gerard appeared to be missing in action. I enquired.

"Where is Gerard?"

"Oh, he is down talking to Mam," my father replied.

"But she is dead," I uttered.

Da looked at me in astonishment and said, as seriously as you like.

"But you can still talk to her."

The next twenty-four hours were like a whirlwind. Everyone kept asking me when I would visit Mam in the morgue. I wanted to remember her as I had seen her in hospital while doing her nails when she was alive. I stuck to my guns until my close friend, Fionuala, arrived. She informed me as the eldest child, I would have to lead the family prayers before the coffin lid was closed. Shocked to the core by this news, I relented and did visit. I regretted the decision for a long time.

My sister Therese had the wake in her house in Cremore and gave Mam a wonderful send-off. Before I left, she hugged me and said.

"Marie, do not stop coming over just because Mam is no longer with us."

I have never forgotten those words. Thank you, sis. After the Wake, I came back to Purley, and life continued.

Oak Lodge was having a new school built on the same site. It was exciting but challenging. The children had to be taught, the staff had to manage, and the architects and builders had to deliver.

Reflecting on this time, Katherine and Alison were busy getting on with their lives. I loved seeing them, whether alone, with friends or partners. They were my priority, and I tried to dilute Howard's antics as much as possible. It was not by any means all doom and gloom between Howard and me. We were good pals and still did lots together. The caravan was a fantastic bolthole for us. We went to the theatre in Chichester a lot, which we loved. We also went for long walks on the South Downs and did plenty of cycling. Not to mention the odd cricket match at Lords and The Oval.

Losing my Mam was a massive event in my life. She had always been there for me, and then she wasn't. I had grieved whilst she was still alive as she had been unwell for so many years; nonetheless, it left a vast hole. Mam, you were a terrific role model for me. Thank you.

I was so grateful Nellie was home to look after Da, as I knew how devastated he would be without Mam. They were totally devoted to each other.

Life continued with Gerard, who was still living in the family home with Da and Nellie. I continued to visit when I could. Da and I became closer. He was very worried about Gerard, who was still hell-bent on self-destruction. Da didn't want to go out much, so we would discuss everything. He was very well-informed and would chat about a wide range of issues. From the price of eggs to the latest position in Russia.

After a few years, Nellie dropped a bombshell and said she was leaving. Disaster. What on earth would happen? I don't think anybody thought she would go, but she did. Fortunately, she found an apartment nearby and looked after Da and Gerard from afar. It worked remarkably well.

However, Da was totally lost without Mam, and it was difficult to watch his demise. The brunt of the situation and all it entailed fell upon my sister Therese. She had the day-to-day management of the whole situation. Gerard was on his slow destruction path, which affected the entire family. He had mental issues plus an alcohol problem. Colman was in France, estranged from his wife and two boys.

Michael was marvellous. He lived in Limerick and, by this time, had become an eminent scientist in his field of smoke alarms. Michael was the Co-owner of a large factory employing hundreds of workers. Fortunately, he followed a very successful career path, unlike our two brothers. He and his wife Patricia have two sons, and whenever possible, he visited Dublin to see Da, Nellie and Gerard.

Michael is a fantastic human being and one of the humblest people I know. He is the anchor every family needs and has been the glue between all his siblings. He had literally been there for each of us over the years. Thank you so much, Michael.

Da lived for nearly six years after Mam. He was in and out of the hospital and ended up in the hospice in Dublin.

Again, before he died, I was privileged enough to chat with him about how things would pan out after he had gone.

He asked me to ensure Colman and Gerard were alright. I told him frankly and honestly that he and Mam had been trying to do it all their lives without too much success. I pointed out that Therese, Michael, and I would unlikely succeed where they had failed. He took this on board, and I was happy that an unrealistic responsibility was not placed on our shoulders.

Da died a few months after this conversation in January 1997.

My Irish and immediate family have always been very important to me and greatly influenced my view of life.

After the business of visiting my Mam's body, I had a few conversations with my sister Therese, categorically stating I was not doing the same with Da. She was brilliant and arranged for him to have a net over his face (tastefully done, may I say), which worked for me. The lead-up to his funeral was much less frenetic than it had seemed for Mam's send-off. He was taken to the church to rest overnight as is customary. We had the funeral Mass the next day, followed by burial in the famous plot discussed over the breakfast table all those years ago with Gran Byrne (my Mam) and my girls.

The grave had six places, and Mam went in first. Logically, Da would go in beside her. Unfortunately, he was rather a large man and needed two spaces! This caused quite a lot of hilarity at the time. Larger in life and death!

By this time, the family home in Dublin had been sold to buy another house opposite where Therese lived. The thinking was it would be easier for her to do the caring. In fact, Da never spent a night there as his last few months were in the hospice.

Gerard continued to rattle around in the house for a while after Da's death. While Colman was steered gently towards the airport to ensure he returned to France after the funeral. The last thing we needed as a family was for those two brothers to hook up. They were a lethal cocktail together.

Da had left all his affairs in apple-pie order, allowing Therese, Michael, and I the wherewithal to attempt to find solutions for our two wayward siblings.

Losing both parents was far more emotional than I thought it would be. After all, we had not lived in the same country for nearly thirty years, so I wasn't expecting the great loss I felt. Over the years, I hadn't overly bothered either of them with my problems, but I always knew they were on the end of a phone. I got my sense of adventure from Da and my caring side from Ma. How lucky am I?

But now, I must move on. I am discovering new things and having new adventures.

FOOTNOTE

The contents of this memoir spanning my middle years are as I remember them. I have tried to be as accurate as possible. It has been a fantastic experience, and I am never bored knowing I can scribble anytime.

I aim to continue writing an account of the next part of my story and hope to God I have learned from my earlier mistakes and become more organised.

Al-Anon Family Groups UK & Eire

We are there for anyone whose life has been affected by someone else's drinking.

Contact details:

Website: https://al-anonuk.org.uk/

Tel. UK – 088 0086 811

Tel Eire – 01 873 2699

From 10 am – 10 pm 365 days a year

ABOUT THE AUTHOR

Born in Dublin, Ireland, I moved to London in the last '60s, where I married and had two daughters. We lived in the Southeast, and I studied to become a teacher, making it to my first classroom in the '70s.

Teaching is in my blood. Living life is in my nature.

Printed in Great Britain
by Amazon